MAINTAINING
THE
SPIRIT
OF
PLACE

MAINTAINING THE SPIRIT OF PLACE

A PROCESS FOR THE PRESERVATION OF TOWN CHARACTER

Harry Launce Garnham

PDA Publishers Corporation
Mesa, Arizona

Library of Congress Cataloging in Publication Data

Garnham, Harry Launce, 1941-
　　Maintaining the spirit of place.

　　Bibliography: p.
　　Includes index.
　　1. Gentrification.　2. Architecture – Conservation and
restoration.　3. City planning – Case studies.
I. Title.
HT170.G37　1985　　　　363.6'9　　　　84-26646
ISBN 0-914886-29-0

PDA PUBLISHERS CORPORATION
1725 East Fountain
Mesa, Arizona 85203

To my mother, Sue Buck Boyt,
for her encouragement and support.

ACKNOWLEDGEMENTS

I wish to acknowledge the various people, programs, and agencies which have given support to this project during its evolution. Support for early text development was provided by the National Endowment for the Arts in Washington, D.C., a Federal agency, for an individual academic and professional research grant. Support for the Navasota, Texas, Case Study was made possible by a grant from the National Endowment of the Arts to Navasota, Texas and by support from Texas A&M University. People helpful to this Navasota project included Raymond Reed, Dean, and Don Austin, Head of Landscape Architecture at Texas A&M University and the following students: Allison Dickson, Dennis Jerke, Dorthy Pautz, Penny Cialone, Ratna Dharia, Tim Hansen, Kay Hutmacher, Bruce Smith, Claire Taylor, Cynthia Cash, and especially Priscilla Floca. The various case studies which developed the foundation for this work would not have happened without the support of students at Harvard, the University of Virginia, Texas A&M University, and Louisiana State University; who, while too numerous to mention individually, played an important role.

A special thanks goes to the faculty of the Harvard Graduate School of Design for their award of the Jacob Weidenman Prize, and to the Loeb Fellowship in advanced environmental studies at Harvard, which provided the opportunity to continue the work which was started during my Weidenmen award travels in Europe.

People who have helped along the way are also numerous, however several stand out because of their continued support, teaching, and encouragement. They are: John Simonds, Kevin Lynch, Stewart Udall, Edward Sekler, Carl Steinitz, and David Woodcock. Special thanks also goes out to Betty Hill, Bob and Jenny Baker, and Dick Reid for showing me England during an important time in the process. I would also like to acknoledge Lane Marshall, Head of Landscape Architecture at Texas A&M University and Ted Walker of PDA Publishers for their support and encouragement in completing this manuscript.

Finally I would like to acknowledge Penny Garnham, who despite her own professional committments, organized and processed the manuscript for final submission; and Caire Lucus who typed early drafts on the road from Instanbul to Kealakekua Bay.

In the final analysis, however, I wrote the words, took the photographs, and assume full responsibility for the final contents.

Harry Launce Garnham

contents

preface

The search for special places and the joy of experiencing special places has been a personal preoccupation since an early time. Seeking to understand those places, and to understand what makes them special, has been a continuing professional preoccupation for 25 years. This activity has resulted in many miles of travel. Travel for the most part to destinations which were identified in books, journals, lectures, artistic expressions, and personal conversations as special places to visit and from which to learn. Many of these places did not live up to my expectations, as time had changed their appearance and their apparent value as a learning experience. Shocked and disappointed at first, I soon began to realize that this was the natural order of things. I realized that change placed new demands upon places, that they could not remain constant in form or function; but as artifacts they had to change to serve new needs.

This realization did not lessen my sense of loss, but created a desire to seek ways to understand what the basic elements were that made these places special, what could be learned from their juxtaposition, and how these elements might be preserved. I began to realized that, despite change, many of these places still expressed their original Genius Loci, or *spirit of place*. This spirit was often the result of constants such as topography, vegetation, visible water, climate, cultural expressions which solved functions in proper relationship to natural conditions, and the resulting visual and sensual expression which was created. Frequently it was **the disruption** of this visual spectrum which became the most readily apparent, a disruption caused by the discordant physical appearance of change, not by change per se. I observed that the places (regions, cities, towns, and town parts i.e., waterfronts, plazas, parks, architectural groupings) which had understood their special aspects, and hand directed change to recognize those aspects, were the most successful in maintaining their *spirit of place*.

I also found that my reactions to a place were based upon personal expectations and motivations, which were often out of balance with the needs, expectations, and motivations of a place's inhabitants. I soon realized that without active participation from a place's people, and an understanding of their needs, no effort toward planned change and preservation of character would be successful.

This book will organize these perceptions into a process designed to maintain the character and spirit of one type of special place, **the small town.** I have found the small town to be uniquely vulnerable to the loss of character created by change; while often also being the most in need of the elements of change, economic progress, and increased cultural and social opportunity. This dilemma has often resulted in an over balance for "progress," without an understanding of the total range of "quality of life costs" to the local population. This conflict, and its potential resolution by citizens, professionals, and students, is the focus of this book.

A key thought concerning the preservation process expressed in this book is that "the basic purpose of preservation is not to arrest time but to mediate sensitively with the forces of change. It is to understand the present as a product of the past and a modifier of the future."[1]

A final note concerns my experience of many special places and the results of that experience upon my professional development. I believe that no design or planning process can exist without its

participants having gained the maximum amount of "place" experiences. These experiences can be directed to a specific task or just exist as a compendium of information waiting for the intuitive connection which will allow them to be utilized in a proper manner. These experiences have provided inspiration for such projects as a memorial plaza in Texas, based upon the memory of morning light striking a ceremonial arch deep in the Yucatan and a plan for the preservation of open space in Hawaii based upon an old Hawaiian woman's explanation of the ancient Hawaiian concept of land utilization. It is my hope that in its ways this book may help preserve both place and the experience of place for future generations of residents and visitors alike.

Santa Fe, New Mexico, USA
November 1984

[1] John W. Lawrence, Dean, School of Architecture Tulane University, New Orleans. April 24, 1970.

(top) A classic example of positive cultural reaction to the landscape and its resulting visual expression.

(bottom) A rich mixture of activities can provide important town image.

introduction

The concept of uniqueness is often illusive and very difficult to clearly express or define when it concerns a specific place. Throughout the world, however, exist places which people categorize as unique and the mention of them can bring forth strong mental images of a remembered or imagined character.

We have assigned values to these places, and these values have manifested themselves in creative works which express the place and create a desire to visit or return to them. We only need to view the photography of Ansel Adams, read Lawrence Durrell, enjoy the poetry of Frost, view the painting of Paul Gaugin, or enjoy the color slides of a tourist just returned to see human expressions of perceived uniqueness or *spirit of place*.

While these and other works have sought to promote, explain, record, protect, enhance, or stand in awe, they all share the common belief that there exists a special uniqueness of each place which can be identified, understood, and communicated to others.

Places such as the South of France; the English Cotswolds; the Shenandoah Valley of Virginia; the Texas Hill Country; Paris; Istanbul; Positano; Santa Fe, New Mexico; Taxco; the Greek Islands; and Hanalei are regions, cities, and towns which possess recognized uniqueness or *spirit of place*.

Places such as these are commonly accepted as special; however, the attention they receive often overshadows the fact that each and every place has some measure of unique expression or quality. An important aspect of this book is its argument that all places have some special aspects, and need not

have worldwide acclaim to justify concern for their protection from the impact of deleterious change. Each of these places will contain locally special attributes which produce a *spirit of place*, and a sense of belonging and well being among a place's people. The ingredients which produce these attributes are based upon: (1) Aspects of the existing natural environment such as land form and topography, vegetation, climate, and the presence of water; (2) cultural expressions such as bridges, forts, or hilltop churches which are a reaction to landscape, social history, physical location, human activities, and place as a cultural artifact (a place's meaning beyond its physical expression such as Yorktown, Virginia, due to its historical significance); and (3) the sensory experience, primarily visual, which results from the interaction of culture with the existing landscape. The holistic interaction of the ingredients which produce a place's attributes are frequently not understood by the local population until they have been unalterably lost; and are, therefore, very vulnerable to unplanned change.

An unfortunate reality is that many of these special places have undergone rapid change as a result of such activities as industrialization, real estate speculation, transportation expansion, urban growth, shifts in population, and organized tourism.[1] This change has altered image, character, and even meaning as the original attributes which gave a place its character have been destroyed or altered. While much of the change is positive, perhaps even required for economic revitalization, it has often happened to the detriment to the original character of the place in which it has occurred.

This book will address this series of issues and how these issues relate to small towns. The book will propose that with awareness, and systematic analysis, a town can begin to identify and define its component ingredients and to accurately communicate the role they play in the creation of its unique character. The book will show that these ingredients tend to be drawn from the town's built form, its natural setting, the activities which happen in it, its past, and the meaning the place has acquired or developed for those who experience it, or have experienced it throughout history.

The book's primary purpose is to provide the knowledge, and a process designed to employ that knowledge, which is required to prevent undesirable town change. This process is designed to encourage the development of plans and programs to facilitate town preservation, revitalization, and maintenance of special character. The concern for this issue is heightened by the continuing loss, or threat of loss, to critical image and character in towns throughout the world environment. Items in many journals, newspapers, and television reports frequently speak to this concern and indicate the importance of, and the critical need for, a process which will help alleviate this trend.[2]

(top) Concern for the relationship of the town to its countryside is very important to the maintenance of town image.

(middle) Historical image can be maintained by the use of compatible materials and allowing critical building groups to remain dominant.

(bottom) The classic small town image can be maintained with planned growth and change.

2

(top left) The dual activities of tourism and fishing give this town its special character.

(middle) Despite seasonal traffic congestion, town character is maintained by the use of consistent architectural style, materials, and modest signage.

(bottom) Town location and function are often the major contributors to Genius Loci.

(top right) Unique architecture provides an indication of cultural variations and their response to climate and local materials.

GOALS – The book's major goals for addressing this critical issue are:

☐ To encourage people to **recognize** and **appreciate** the unique character of their towns, the **Genius Loci.**

☐ To provide a planning process by which citizen activity can help maintain desired town quality and character.

☐ To encourage citizens to become actively involved, working in concert with professionals, in the planning and implementation process for their town.

☐ To facilitate these goals the book outlines: A citizen participation oriented planning and design process directed toward the concerned laymen; the suggested role of the practicing planning and design professional in the process; and a focused process which, aided by the bibliography, will facilitate the education of planning and design students.

CHAPTER ONE introduces the basic philosophical background of the book and speaks to the notions of *spirit of place* and change as they relate to small town preservation, revitalization and the maintenance of essential character.

CHAPTER TWO outlines a specific process designed to create a plan and program for the preservation, revitalization, and maintenance of small town character, *spirit of place*, and quality of life, while allowing economic development and growth to occur.

CHAPTER THREE constitutes a case study which indicates how the methodology was applied in a series of places and a specific small town.

It has been suggested that: "No society racing through the turbulence of the next several decades will be able to do without specialized centers in which the rate of change is artificially depressed. To phrase it differently, we shall need enclaves of the past; communities in which turn over, novelty and choice are deliberately limited."[3] The fervent hope of this book is that through the use of its suggested planning and design process the need for such "specialized centers" will be eliminated or vastly reduced and that town quality and *spirit of place* can be maintained as a product of normal, but directed, growth and change.

WHO BENEFITS

Looking briefly at who might benefit from such activities we find:

☐ **The town's people**, through better quality of life, more diversity and choice in public space and activity, understanding of history and its role in community image and meaning, and pride in community;

(top) Neglect may alter town image as seriously as improper growth and change.

(bottom) Much of a town's character is provided by human activity; places for this activity to happen should be maintained.

(top) Distinctive architectural expression can produce a strong sense of place for a town or region.

(bottom) The interaction between citizens and professionals is critical throughout the process of creating a Town Uniqueness Preservation Plan.

□ **Commercial and business concerns**, through long-term financial gains, high self-image, leadership in community revitalization, potential access to low interest loans tied to a revitalization plan, knowledge that aesthetics is good business, and the creation of a community where preservation and revitalization are part of all citizens' daily lives;

□ **City government and public leaders**, through the creation of a long-term tax base, a desirable place for people to live and invest, community distinction, pride, and high quality of life.

FOCUS

The focus of this book will be towns with a population under 10,000 people, without an organized planning office or staff, and not having a comprehensive plan. Medium sized towns with comprehensive plans or larger populations can also benefit from the proposed process; however, towns with ongoing comprehensive planning activities or larger populations may need to modify the process to suit their specific situation. Many comprehensive plans often do not include a sensitivity to the preservation of town character or quality of town life. One of the primary reasons for this book was the fact that the implementation of many comprehensive plans destroyed much of the character and *spirit of place* enjoyed by towns prior to planning activities, despite the fact that comprehensive planning was often the proper path. A major function of the book is to provide towns without comprehensive planning programs a structure within which to plan for future growth and change, before it occurs, therefore preventing loss of essential town character. This structure will also provide the direction needed to ensure that future comprehensive planning, if it occurs, will respect overall town image and quality.

PROCESS

The process suggested by this book was designed to remain flexible with use and not become rigid methodology. Each town will develop its own exact process and each group of citizens and professionals will often need to make adaptations suited to the specific task at hand. The process does, however, establish a frame of reference within which the project's purpose can be realized.

A rapidly emerging national trend, based upon the 1980 census, indicates that large numbers of people are moving to small and medium size towns on a permanent or part-time basis. Many of these people are seeking a quality of life which is increasingly lacking in major urban centers. All indications are that this general shift to small and medium size towns will continue to increase and include a growing number of younger, as well as older, people. This trend underscores the need for planning and design activities such as those which will be outlined in this book; as, much of the quality of life these people seek may be **lost** due to the **impact of their arrival**.[4] Of particular concern to towns is that, "Conclusive ... evidence has been developed during the past five years that quality of life is not a frill, but is one of the essential competitive resources to be managed by communities for their own economic well being in the decades of the 80's and 90's."[5] And finally, each town must realize that "*Sense of place* is not a fine art extra; it is something we can not afford to do without."[6]

1.1 *Genius Loci,* or spirit of place, *is often created by the mixture of function, art, architecture, and people's activities in public space.*

1.2 *Cultural reaction to landscape can provide an outstanding example of town uniqueness.*

1.1

1.2

1

spirit of place

GENIUS LOCI

This book proposes a design and planning process which incorporates the notion of "Genius Loci," the *spirit of place*, as that concept relates to town preservation and revitalization. This notion is based upon the belief that each town has its own individual special uniqueness, character, indentity, and *spirit* which differs from all other places. A spirit which has value and meaning to a town's inhabitants, and without which their quality of life would be diminished.

It is important that the citizens and planning/design professionals undertaking the process outlined in Chapter Two understand the basic concept of "Genius Loci" and include that awareness within each step of the process.

Early in the process, project participants should become familiar with portions of the extensive resource material available on the notion of "Genius Loci" and that concept's relationship to town character identification. The following sampler of quotations were selected to assist in this familiarization process. *Norberg-Schulz* has written extensively upon this notion and reinforces this book's theme when he says, "We will recall the old concept of 'Genius Loci.' Since remote times man has recognized that different places have a different character. This character is often so strong that it, in fact, determines the basic properties of the environmental images of most people present, making them feel that they experience and belong to the same place."[7] When these images are altered, destroyed, or otherwise removed from people's daily lives the essential bond between person and place can be broken, with a subsequent tangible loss in the basic quality of life. This phenomenon is not localized to one region or culture, but has been shown to persist on a worldwide scale. *Rene Dubos*

states that, "The widespread acceptance of the words 'Genius' and 'Spirit' to denote the distinctive characteristics of a given region or city implies the tacit acknowledgement that each place possesses a set of attributes that determines the uniqueness of its landscape and its people."[8] The focus of this book's concern is that this "set of attributes" not be the casualty of town change, but are instead recognized for their value and incorporated into the decision making process. *Alexander Pope* said, "Consult the Genius of the Place in all."[9] The popular interpretation of this statement is, "... that local topography, climate, and resources determine the kind of Landscape and Architecture which is best suited to a particular region."[10] The primary concern, therefore, is to isolate the major components of a place's identity of *spirit*, and then divide these components into logical ingredient sets for future decision making activities. To do this we must accept the notion that each place has a definable character, *spirit*, and identity; and we must then apply that attitude to the preservation and revitalization process.

The major components of identity have been found to be:

1. **Phsycial Features and Appearance**
   The actual physical structure of a place. The reality of its buildings, landscape, climate and aesthetic quality.

2. **Observable Activities and Functions**
   How a place's people interact with it, how their cultural institutions have affected it, and how the buildings and landscapes are used.

3. **Meanings or Symbols**
   A more complex aspect, primarily the result of human intentions and experiences. Much of a place's character will be derived from peoples reaction to its physical and functional aspects.[11]

It is the complicated interaction between these primary components which creates "Genius Loci," and it is this interaction which must be understood to successfully undertake preservation and revitalization activities in small town environments.

The level of a person's understanding, as to the role these above listed items play in determining definition of *sense of place*, is often based upon the degree of familiarity a person has with the place. Each participant will approach the project with a different background; a different set of personal experiences, attitudes, and memories; a different individual focus; and each will have a different reaction to their immediate sensation of the town. An understanding of this basic situation is required by all participants, as they must strive to move toward a common consensus. People from inside the town must realize that there will be variations in their views and perceptions. Team members from outside the town must also be aware that the attitudes they bring with them must be modified to better suit their purpose for being there.

The following notions are based upon information developed by anthropologists to distinguish the extent to which a person is assimilated into an unfamiliar culture or place, and are provided here to assist project participants in obtaining their proper relationship to the town and its citizens.

Behavioral – engaging in the activities of the culture while remaining a dispassionate observer.

Empathetic – involving emotional as well as behavioral participation, while retaining an awareness of not being a full member of the culture or place.

Cognitive or "Going Native" – in which it ceases to be possible to study a culture or place. This is the stage to be avoided by all project participants.

The reader should keep in mind that the goal of this whole effort is to identify the *spirit* of a place and the components of that *spirit* as the **citizens** of a place perceive it, and incorporate the information into plans and programs for town preservation, revitalization, and character maintenance.

The persons helping the town's citizens in this effort, in particular Team members, will often be outsiders who must strive to become "empathetic." The citizens who represent various levels of "insideness" must strive to develop enough perspective to assist in the creation of a meaningful plan. It is mandatory, therefore, that project particpants strive to understand the importance of walking the fine line between the dispassionate observer, and becoming so involved that comprehensive perspective is lost. The creation of group consensus, therefore, is critical to project success, and requires that all participants approach the project with a common point of reference.[12]

1.3

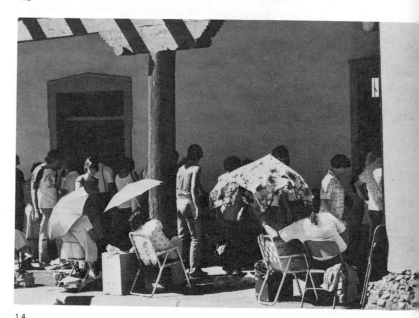
1.4

1.3 Unique identity is often a factor of consistent architectural style and visable activities.

1.4 Activities which encourage tourism and provide revenue for town citizens create positive image and character.

1.5

1.6

1.5 *Outstanding visual images are often the result of architecture, landscape, and preservation legislation.*

1.6 *Unique architecture often is an indication of cultural diversity and history. Symbols provide meaning beyond physical expression.*

CHANGE

Town character is often irretrievably altered by major growth and change as well as minor, daily decisions. The loss of essential town character, however, is often not noticed by local populations until it has occurred, and until the impact of their daily decisions are compounded to forever change the very nature of the town they inhabit.

The identification of unique character must preceed change, and change must be designed to accommodate the preservation of that uniqueness. If this is done, tremendous superficial growth and change can occur without altering the major components which make up a town's baseline character. The desired level of historic continuity, growth and economic development, therefore, can be accomplished without destroying essential town quality.

Unique character, or strong sense of place is often based upon such items as:

☐ Architectural Style

☐ Climate, particularly the quality and quantity of light, amount of rainfall, and variations in temperature.

☐ Unique natural setting

☐ Memory and metaphor, what the place means to people who experience it.

☐ The use of local materials

☐ Craftsmanship

☐ Sensitivity in the siting of important buildings and bridges

☐ Cultural diversity and history

☐ People's values

☐ High quality public environments which are visible and accessible.

☐ Townwide activities daily and seasonal

These items, which are expanded in Chapter Two, represent an initial breakdown of the range of possible local conditions which: Create a unique town spirit or character; separate one place from another; and begin to introduce more detail to the three previously mentioned basic character components: Physical Features and Appearance; Observable Activities and Functions; and Meanings or Symbols.[13]

Growth and change, however, have often introduced a regrettable sameness to many towns – a sameness which has eroded their individual qualities and destroyed their unique character. The symbols of sameness are represented by unsightly and inappropriate signs, traffic congestion created by poor planning, franchise architecture, noxious industrial development, the thoughtless juxtaposition and poor design of gas stations, fastfood chains, shopping centers, land use patterns, highways, and public buildings that one encounters in every region and town. This development is not harmful because it is development; it is harmful because of the often insensitive imposition of a foreign character upon an existing town without recognizing what the town's special character is, and what type of town image the town's people want. Development of this type and the loss of vital character, often a product of rapid growth and change, has become a critical international problem. Change of this nature places an undue strain upon a town, its people, and its surrounding region. This strain seriously affects the town's ability to absorb growth, and still retain the character, scale and other attributes which were the roots of its original attractiveness.

Many factors may stimulate change, and, as in the case of rapid growth, often include much needed and desirable economic vitality. The requirement, therefore, is not to stop growth and change; but to mitigate its negative impact on town environments. Factors contributing to change, the introduction of sameness, and the potiential loss of character are as varied as the regions of the world and might include such items as: sudden changes in zoning, tax structures, and land ownership; proposed mineral extraction; industrial, residential, recreational, or tourist development at a massive scale; the creation of a lake or other major attraction; the location of a major expressway or interchange; the extension of metropolitan transportation service; shifting population trends (such as the rapid migration to the U.S. sunbelt during the later 20th century); and real estate speculation accelerating at a fantastic pace in newly accessible small towns and highly desirable, unique town environments. Due to the impacts of these conditions, and to the lack of proper planning in anticipation of the pressures of change, towns which possess a high degree of identity and character are fast disappearing from the world landscape.

FOCUS

The major desire of this book, as stated in the introduction, is to present a process which incorporates an empathy for small town "Genius Loci" and recognizes that each town has its own important uniqueness and *spirit of place*. This process, which is heavily dependent upon citizen participation and energy, identifies the ingredients of town character and provides a method to guide town growth and change while maintaining town character. The goal of this process is to foster local planning and design decision making before development pressure or continued neglect forces irreversible change, while also allowing needed economic growth to occur.

1.7

1.8

1.9

1.10

1.11

1.7 *Image and character can be destroyed by the thoughtless use of signs and trite architecture in historic settings.*

1.8 *The blandness and visual disruption of franchise architecture has ruined the character and spirit of countless towns.*

1.9 *A strong visual landmark will help organize the image of the street and help reduce the impacts of change.*

1.10 *Historic structures provide a town with unique character and a connection with the past.*

1.11 *Unique image is often created by the proper relationship between landscape and structures.*

1.12 *Water and art in public places have historically created a spirit of place and provided strong metaphors.*

1.12

While much of the process is concerned with existing spirit, and its maintenance, it also recognizes that growth and change require the creation of new images and new character. To be successful however, these new images should occur within the context of an overall plan and program for each town. It is the negative impact of growth which the process is designed to minimize. The design of positive new images, however, is a vital aspect of the ongoing activity of town preservation and revitalization and when properly executed will add to overall character and quality of life. Chapter Two describes a process designed to encourage a town's citizens to become aware of their town's unique aspects, its "Genius Loci," and how they can become involved in organizing the information into a plan and program which will guide future growth and change in a positive manner. The initial burden of making the decision to undertake the process will fall upon concerned citizens and will be dependent upon their energy and willingness to actively participate in the entire process.

The process is designed to function with maximum citizen participation, however a Team of professionals will be required to undertake much of the actual project. Concerned citizens in each town undertaking the process outlined in this book should determine, by study of this book's contents, what level of professional assistance would be required to undertake the tasks which are recommended. Each small town will contain citizens with various expertise useful to the project and who may be willing to participate on the actual project Team. The process was designed to be conducted by a Team which includes planning and design professionals and selected community members. The mix will be dependent upon local resources, and will vary from Teams with no local residents to Teams which are predominately local residents. Chapter Two suggests how the Team might originate and how the actual project would begin

One feature of the process is that undertaking this process need not require extensive use of a town's limited financial resources. Town citizens can determine how much professional expertise is required; if it needs to be full-time or part-time; and when in the process, it would be most useful. A town, for instance, with local volunteer professionals making up the Team may only need to hire selected additional professional participation. This situation will vary with place; however, the Team mix must include sufficient planning and design professionals from the very beginning to ensure project success.

An additional, unique, and important aspect of this process is that each phase results in a discrete and useful product. This feature allows the town to obtain a useful product during the process and also prevents much wasted effort should the entire process never be completed.

1.13

1.14

1.15

12

The overriding hope of this book is that each town will use the process to develop a plan and program to maintain its unique attributes while pursuing a concept of quality growth. This program should be fully be supported by an informed and involved citizenry and be in complete empathy with the *spirit of place.*

1.16

1.17

1.13 *The use of local materials and craftsmanship often provide a strong sense of place.*

1.14 *Town uniqueness is often derived from a functional need like crossing a river.*

1.15 *Historic artifacts indicate a place's past culture and function.*

1.16 *Quality towns should have open space which is visible and accessible to many activities.*

1.17 *Activity, planned or spontaneous, provides a key ingredient for quality images within a town.*

PROCESS

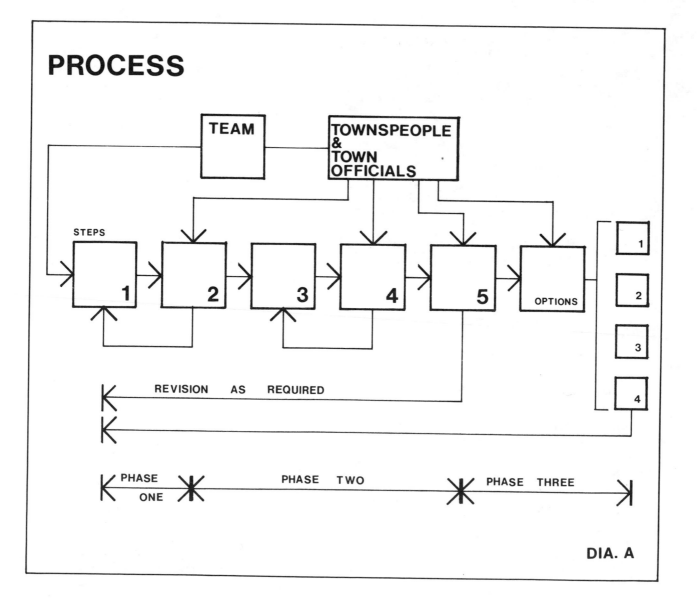

DIA. A

2

process

Identifying and maintaining the spirit or character of a place requires an organized and flexible process. The major concern in presenting a process designed to complete this task is that it be easily understood and have as its general function the ability to be continuously updated and revised.

The data required to articulate town uniqueness are not static, but always in flux. Therefore any mapping or visual display system is always subject to revision and while some aspects to town uniqueness are fixed, many will need regular revision. Accepting this fact, the process suggested in this chapter has a continuous sequence of **monitor, feedback,** and **revision** as it moves toward its objective of facilitating the maintenance of town quality while allowing for community change.

Diagram "A" illustrates the three PHASES. Five Steps, four options and points of major citizen participation being suggested. **PHASE ONE** consists of a series of initial activities; a research component and a set of inventory tasks. This phase results in an initial statement of town uniqueness and special character. **PHASE TWO** consists of an expanded and very specific inventory and analysis task which requires extensive mapping of data and sensitive evaluation of that information. Phase Two is concluded by the synthesis of this information into the **Town Uniqueness Preservation Plan** which is the heart of this entire process. The **OPTION PHASE**, builds upon the base of the Town Uniqueness Preservation Plan through creative planning and design. This option indicates how the results of the Town Uniqueness Preservation Plan

might be incorporated into a town's ongoing development. A unique aspect of the entire process is that each phase suggests a system of participation designed to continuously monitor and update the results. This allows for constant feedback and provides for continuous revision opportunities as conditions change.

A major factor to remember is the stance taken by this type of planning. A stance which says that the entire effort is designed to locate town uniqueness, identify the ingredients of that uniqueness, place values upon their composite characteristics, and organize them to facilitate their preservation or sensitive enhancement as a component of firm and enlightened public and private policy. This process is not designed to execute a comprehensive master plan but to determine what is special about a place and encourage comprehensive planning, and resultant town growth, to defer to the specialness. The major fault of many comprehensive planning efforts is that they fail to recognize uniqueness and do not defer to the special qualities of a place. The process presented here, however, indicates the various tasks required to conduct a town study which will recognize the need to include this key information into any town planning endeavor. Numerous case studies, however, indicate that all towns and organizations do not possess the time, resources or ability to conduct the entire process being presented in this book. Therefore, the process has been broken into phases which will render a useful product at the end of each phase and require a consensus commitment from town citizens before the next phase is undertaken.

2.1

2.1 *The illusive spirit of historic places is similar to that spirit of place, or Genius Loci, which we are seeking to identify in town environments.*

2.2 *Despite its age and ruinous condition this town's spirit of place is very well defined. The care used in its designed relationship to its site, organization of functions, and concern for visual orientation still permeates one's experience of this place.*

PHASE ONE

PHASE ONE deals with process Steps One and Two and is designed to get the project underway. **PHASE ONE GOALS** are as follows:

☐ Establish a study Team to undertake a town preservation and revitalization study.

☐ Inform and educate the town's citizens concerning the project.

☐ Organize a group of citizens to work with the study Team.

☐ Conduct research and inventory.

☐ Produce a statement, supported by the town's citizens, articulating general town uniqueness and character.

STEP ONE consists of the initial organizational aspects of the project.

STEP TWO indicates how the initial statement of town uniqueness is obtained and recorded.

During the first step, a relationship is established between a town and the Team who will undertake the effort. Each town study will vary in its initial organization but central to all efforts is the expressed concern by some group that the town in question has a certain level of "uniqueness" or "specialness" which needs identification, and a program to protect, or enhance, this uniqueness while it undergoes physical and social change. The following examples indicate how other projects have started and indicates the various people who can create the final results:

1. Concerned citizens within a community can recognize the problems their town is facing and organize both resources and personal commitment toward a suitable alternative course of action. Groups such as this may undertake projects with limited assistance by using the methodology outlined here or by seeking assistance from various organizations. An example is a small town civic club requesting aid from the Agricultural Extension Service who in turn might arrange for assistance from a university-sponsored planning and design Team.[14]

2. University Teams may also initiate town studies. In cases such as this, a town is brought to the attention of concerned university professionals who in turn convince local citizens of the need for preservation and revitalization activities. This technique has the value of being able to provide a wide range of expertise to a community which has resources too limited to employ a professional Team. Projects such as these also provide excellent experience for students and often result in work of very high quality.

3. Special interest firms might also seek to undertake such projects at their own initiative or the initiation of a concerned town or group of

2.2

town citizens. Such firms often are non-profit in their organization and for a limited town investment can provide excellent results.

4. Similar in nature to special interest firms are organizations established within foundations or private funds to undertake planning and design studies in selected regions. They may seek projects or can be sought out by citizens, and have the extra advantage of complete knowledge of the local situation in a given region.

5. Another major resource is the myriad of federal, state and local agencies which are involved in various aspects of planning and design. They may undertake special studies or be able to provide useful assistance in the form of data or specialized manpower. A major advantage of these agencies is their long-term staying power and their ability to relate a town to a broader regional or state wide context. Such agencies as State Planning departments, Councils of Governments, Arts Councils, Soil Conservation Service, County Planning departments, and Regional Planning Commissions serve as examples of this category.

6. Consulting firms of planning and design professionals also become involved in work of the nature described in this book. A town with the financial resources to hire consultants could benefit greatly from the experience. A complete understanding of the book's basic process will be most useful to town citizens and leaders in selecting and working with a consultant.

The cost of consulting services can often be reduced dramatically if a town can organize the project, collect and organize data, and establish clear tasks which need professional attention. Once this is undertaken clear contracts can be drawn and a town can maximize its resources while obtaining a quality product.

State and local chapters of the American Society of Landscape Architects (ASLA), American Institute of Architects (AIA), and American Planning Association (APA) can provide names of qualified consultants. The AIA also provides assistance with the *Regional/Urban Design Assistance Teams (R/UDAT)* program. These Teams may be requested by a local AIA chapter and are made up of volunteer professionals drawn from a national pool.

A new program, also sponsored by the AIA, is the *Urban Design Charette/Seminar Series.* This program is site specific; and is designed to involve local citizens, students, public officials, and design professionals in an intense workshop format. Communities may request this program from the local or national AIA.

Using this organizational material as a guideline, each town in need of assistance should be able to decide which type, or combination of types, of project Team it wants to obtain and how it is to be funded.

2.3 Unique towns are often a product of landscape, architectural style, and development controls.

2.4 *Classic small town spirit of place is created by many elements which coalesce over time into a harmonius expression of site, culture, and visual quality.*

STEP ONE –
THE STUDY TEAM AND INITIAL
WORKSHOPS

In whatever manner the project is set up a Team of people will be established to conduct the actual work, and it is at this point that the process described in this book begins. The Team's actual make up will vary greatly; however, certain basic skills will be required by its composite members. These skills include graphic and verbal communication; photography; mapping; writing; willingness to work with citizens; some knowledge of natural, cultural, and visual systems; knowledge of political, legal, and economic systems; and a capacity for hard work. The level of involvement for each type of expertise in a particular project will depend upon how many phases are undertaken and to what depth. The size of the study Team will also vary and will be determined by these same considerations.

The Team should be selected so that it has the basic planning and design knowledge to undertake

the project. Its members will also be responsible for working with the local participants and providing the direction they will require to undertake selected project aspects. Experience, and other published accounts, have indicated that local citizens functioning as project participants provide extremely useful assistance. The insights they provide and the tasks they can undertake, from workshop participation to inventory assistance, will both enhance and expand the Team's capacity. Prior to starting the project, a Team leader must be chosen.

Once the process begins, total local citizen awareness of its goals should become a major concern for the Team. The Team should conduct workshops designed to communicate the reasons for the effort and how the process is going to work to all citizens. These workshops will vary in format and content, but should stress the **active** participatory role expected of the town's citizens. During these sessions it is essential that all participants understand the concept of **Genius Loci**, as it relates

2.5 *Special towns are often the result of landscape setting, building profiles, activities, and visual composition. An important element is the frequent occurrence of public overlooks which allow views of the town and its setting.*

to this specific task, which was presented in Chapter One. This understanding will establish the philosophical basis for the planning and design effort described throughout this book. In summary this concept holds that the town's character *or spirit of place* will be identified by the community and that its protection and sensitive enhancement will be basic to final plans, programs, recommendations, and implementation ideas.

One suggested aspect of these workshops would be a set of lectures, prepared by the Team, which will clearly establish project purpose and direction. These lectures should include photographic examples of other places and stress the universal nature of towns facing the problems of growth and change. These lectures should include both good and bad examples of change, and how some places have retained their character and how some have lost it. It should also be stressed that economic growth is often desired and that the activities being undertaken by the Team are not designed to stop growth but to manage it in such a

way as to preserve and revitalize town quality. These lecture sessions should focus upon the need for citizens to communicate their values to the Team and stress the fact that throughout the process citizen values will be central to all Team decisions. General workshops should also be conducted as part of Step One and are the best vehicle for obtaining such information as: Citizen hopes for the town; what the town means to them, and what their values are; and what town quality objectives they have. While much of this information is vague, much specific information is also gained. The Team must now organize this information into basic assumptions and project goals. These early assumptions and goals, while tentative and flexible, can begin to provide a frame of reference for initial project organization and future workshop sessions. The workshops should focus upon the town under study and be conducted with the broadest possible cross-section of local citizens. These workshops, combined with lectures, should make the citizens aware of their town and sensitive to the issues involved in the study.

2.6 The rich quality of pedestrian space found in older towns provides a strong spirit of place. The ingredients which produce these spaces can be utilized in the creation of positive new places in revitalized town environments.

THE CITIZEN ADVISORY COMMITTEE

Once these lectures and general workshop sessions are complete, the Team should help form a Citizens Advisory Committee (CAC). Committee members should number about 15 to 20 people and should be drawn from such existing groups as: Service clubs; special interest groups; business and professional leaders; town or county officials; university, community college, and technical school persons; social clubs; and individual, concerned citizens. This committee must assume the role of constant interaction with the study Team and should be chosen with much care. All people chosen for this role must be willing to put forth much time and effort and must be willing to work for the duration of the project.

No attempt should be made to load the committee with people who share common ideas to the exclusion of different points of view. This is often done to avoid conflict and to increase efficiency; however, the price paid for conflict in the early stages is worth the effort when townwide consensus is required for implementation. The Team must realize that **implementation** is the major goal of this project and full support from **all** citizens will be required for successful project completion. To this end the Team should identify the town leaders, the movers and shakers, who have track records for getting things done in the community and ensure that these people become involved in the process.

A major recommendation at this point of committee organization is to hire or appoint a manager. This person will serve as a communication link between the committee and the study Team and will provide continuity once the Team is disbanded. The manager, if one can be hired, should be full-time and should have some background in planning, economics, design, preservation, environmental studies, or political science. A manager can be employed by the town, a citizen's organization, a merchant's association or other appropriate group. The concept of using a manager has been proven with much success by the National Trust for Historic Preservation's "Main Street Program," and will work very well within the context of the process described in this book. A person on the committee should be appointed to function in this manager role in case one is not hired. This task should not be added to the existing city manager's role unless the project manager becomes an assistant city manager funded by the city for this specific task. In either case the manager should be on the Citizen Advisory Committee. The goals of STEP ONE, therefore, are to:

☐ Inform and educate the town's citizens concerning the project.

☐ Obtain a general idea of citizen values.

☐ Determine citizen goals concerning their town and its quality.

2.7

2.8

2.7 *Knowledge of the siting of historic buildings, their orientation, and relationship to context often provide clues to understanding the reasons behind town spirit and character.*

2.8 *Change in this town resulted in its major square being filled with an auto park. The resultant loss of pedestrian space and visual quality is very objectionable.*

22

2.9 Well designed change can provide new functions within town uniqueness areas without destroying essential character.

☐ Create a general statement, which is supported by the citizens, of the study Team's basic assumptions and goals for use in the next step of PHASE ONE.

☐ Create the Citizens Advisory Committee and select a manager.

STEP TWO
INFORMATION GATHERING

Early in STEP TWO the Team should gather general information concerning the town. Working with the Committee, **whose members should in fact help gather information,** the Team should obtain:

☐ Historic social and cultural (i.e. ethnic background) information of the town and the origination of its citizens.

☐ An understanding as to what extent social activity may have influenced the town's character.

☐ A feeling for natural conditions which may have influenced town location i.e. location on a south facing slope or a river crossing.

☐ Economic Data – Specifically information concerning economic base and any current market studies or trend forecasts which may exist.

☐ Political organization – How is the town organized: is it a township or an incorporated town in a county; or just a village subject to county control. The answers will vary from place to place and are very important in deciding how to organize the project, as existing government is a major base for implementation.

☐ Previous planning studies, if they exist, and the names of contact persons in the various agencies conducting planning in the study area.

☐ Level of private sector interest in funding preservation and revitalization projects and private sector knowledge of tax credits from preservation oriented development.

The depth of this background investigation will vary with data availability, budget limitations, and the ability of the citizen's advisory committee to provide assistance; however, it should be completed in an organized manner and retained for future steps in the process.

It should be remembered that this process is designed to identify town uniqueness and that the gathering of data which is not useful to this focus or is gathered in too much detail is often non-productive and can consume valuable time. Obtain only enough information for general understanding of the town's overall background: more detail can be obtained as required by future project demands.

One very helpful task which the Team and the citizens should undertake is to study previous planning and design reports done for other small towns. Reports which deal with special-focus planning will often provide much better examples than traditional, comprehensive planning reports which are often very repetitive. The Team should obtain as many examples as possible; weed out the poor ones; and study the ones which are well organized and communicate the results of the planning effort. These examples will be helpful when the Team begins to collect and organize data and when it organizes conclusions into final form. Items to note are:

☐ Report length and organization

☐ The use of photos, graphs, sketches, charts, maps and diagrams

☐ How the report is bound and what page size is used

☐ The clarity of communication that the text provides

☐ Special features which help the report convince its readers to accept the message

University libraries, government planning office libraries, professional design organization libraries, and organizations such as the National Trust for Historic Preservation will be the best sources for project reports which will provide good examples.

LOOKING AT THE REGION

Basic to STEP TWO is a regional reconnaissance which is required to understand the town's context and the effect of that context upon town character or town change. The Team should conduct this activity in an effort to determine the various subareas of the town's region and the relationship of these subareas to the town being studied. During the reconnaissance field trips, the Team should obtain and record information with photographs, sketches, annotated maps, and notes sufficient enough to describe the region's image and relate that image to town character. This basic inventory should be done in enough detail for understanding, but should not be so indepth that it consumes extensive time or obtains information of limited

usefulness. The idea is for the Team to understand, record, and communicate the basic sense of the region.[15] Just what the limits of a town's region or context might be will vary with each project, however the Team must decide from map investigation, personal observation and discussions with local citizens where the approximate physical and mental boundaries are located. This knowledge will establish the town's context and provide an understanding of its location in the landscape.

Obtaining U.S. Geological Survey maps or aerial photos of the area is most helpful in organizing this effort. Early sensitivity can also be gained by reading local newspapers, listening to radio programs and talking with local people. The information should be organized into a general overview of overall regional character and then refined into the major components of that character: Natural systems; Cultural systems; and Visual systems. These three headings – Natural, Cultural, and Visual – have been selected because they include the entire spectrum of the place identity ingredients described in Chapter One. "Physical features and appearance, observable activities and functions, and meanings or symbols"[16] and have worked successfully in numerous case studies.[17, 18]

NATURAL INFORMATION should include the three following headings which are the basic ingredients of natural character:

☐ *Landform* will include such things as: Steepness of the land and topographic relief; unusual surface features (mesas, cinder cones, drumlins, arroyos); the nature and appearance of surface rock outcroppings; the types of soils (texture, color, diversity); and the general makeup of the land (hills, rivers, flatland or bottomland).

☐ *Vegetation* analysis should include: The amount of land in vegetation; the type (grassland, brush, trees, farm fields, meadows) of vegetation seen and any indications of decay or disease; and any basic ecological relationships which may exist and be observed.

☐ *Water* aspects should be recorded by locating such items as: rivers; falls; lakes; ponds; beaches; marsh; and swamps. Also noted should be the entire drainage pattern, how it effects the land, and what potential for recreation and wildlife habitat might exist.

CULTURAL INFORMATION required to understand how the landscape is being used should be recorded by the Team. Items which should be observed and recorded are:

☐ Public lands, open space and parks

☐ Evidence of agricultural activity of both local and national distribution crops

☐ The general quality of upkeep of farms and ranches

☐ The complexity of land use

2.10

2.11

2.10 *Regional landscape character and unique landscape places provide both context and image for town uniqueness.*

2.11 *Unique landforms can provide important views from town environments. Their preservation is often critical to maintaining the spirit and character of a place.*

☐ Recent, new, land development and in-town projects

☐ Utility systems such as gas, water, electricity, sewers, telephone, cable television, and regional utilities (i.e. natural gas pipelines, electrical transmission lines and microwave towers)

☐ Public infrastructure such as schools, airports, hospitals, governmental offices, police stations, fire stations, transportation networks, and utility easements.

☐ Cherished places such as historic structures, churches, cemeteries, and special monuments.

☐ Landmarks, man-made or natural objects given special meaning by the local or regional population

Of special note should be metropolitan influence on the region such as:

☐ The circulation and transportaion systems and facilities

☐ The location of economic base items such as tourism and industrial facilities

☐ Political boundaries

☐ Population densities and make-up

☐ All types of polluted areas

☐ The effect of physical boundaries (i.e. rivers, hills, mesas, wetlands, etc.) upon development

VISUAL INFORMATION systems are those aspects of the composite natural and cultural landscape which give it much of its character and identity. This entire task is done essentially as a visual reconnaissance with such items noted and recorded as follows:

☐ Viewpoints and what you can see from them

☐ Unique areas having a strong sense of place

☐ Places of interaction phenomenon such as sunsets and rainbows

☐ Locations for experiencing climatic and seasonal change such as Fall color, wildflowers and thunderstorms

☐ Sequence of views and resulting visual delights (Motion is an aspect of this experience.)

☐ Outdoor activities and the visual interest they provide

☐ Visual cues providing a sense of regional identification or place

Particular note should be taken of the item above, the "sequence of views," with special emphasis upon existing view and the changing or emerging view which enhance one another and thus create a prime ingredient and richness in the landscape's visual experience.

This information regarding visual quality allows the Team to understand the potential visual relationships between the town and its context and

2.12

2.13

2.14

2.15

2.16

2.17

2.12 *Agricultural fields provide much of the open space surrounding many towns. Their preservation is critical to maintaining image and economic diversity.*

2.13 *The agricultural production of a region should be understood as an indicator of future, land use trends.*

2.14 *Cultural expressions provide positive image within regional landscapes. As towns grow and change these images should be identified and maintained.*

2.15 *Archaeological artifacts, unless identified and protected, are often destroyed by growth and new land development. Artifacts such as these petroglyphs are very important to the spirit of place.*

2.16 *Commercial activities can provide special visual images.*

2.17 *Regional character is often a major force in understanding a town's uniqueness and its overall context. Phenomena such as tidal and seasonal change create continuous interest in this view looking out from town.*

...e these relationships play in creating town ...acter.

The importance of these visual cues to regional identification is very great, as the Team may be unfamiliar with the study area's landscape and the images which play a major role in determining the character of an area. People and their attitudes are affected by landscape images; therefore, this regional expression is very important to capture and understand. If one just remembers the incredible diversity of the American landscape as seen in Hawaii vs. New England or the Rio Grande Valley vs. the Shenandoah Valley, the importance of this effort to the true understanding of a town should be very clear.

Many very sophisticated techniques exist for undertaking large scale visual analysis and synthesis; however, these techniques are time consuming, often require extensive training to undertake, and would provide more information than a town study will require. While these techniques are not recommended for this effort the reader may find the many references in this book's bibliography helpful should one want to conduct a more sophisticated visual assessment.

LOOKING AT THE TOWN more specifically should occur simultaneously with the regional, visual reconnaissance. The Team should obtain and record their initial impression of the town, its basic physical structure, and its physical image. A suggested approach is to record this information with drawings, photographs (color transparencies and black & white), notes, and annotated maps. For this activity the Team must obtain or produce an accurate, plan map of the town as it currently exists. Maps are often available at City Hall, the Chamber of Commerce, or office supply stores. The map should include:

☐ Highways and streets

☐ Railroads

☐ Major street names

☐ Subdivision names

☐ Grade separations

☐ Major drainage ways

☐ Bodies of water

☐ Easements

☐ Town limit line

If no complete map exists, one may be created from aerial photographs. These photographs may often be economically obtained from highway department files, town or county tax office, the U.S. Soil Conservation Service, the County Agricultural Extension agent, NASA, or from commercial stock mapping companies. Once a map is created from one of these sources it can be enlarged to a proper size, perhaps 1" = 400' or 1" = 200' depending upon the town's size.

2.18

2.19

2.18 Maintaining the spirit of towns and their settings often requires that new development defer to the scale, materials, and compactness of existing development.

2.19 The unfortunate placement of signs at this town's entry point provides an unpleasant first impression.

2.20

This initial information is required to complete the tasks in Phase One of the process; and if well executed, will provide much of the information required for Phase Two and potential Phase Three activities. Using the following organizational framework the Team should record the following suggested information for the town:

1. The town's **visual setting** within its region should be explained. Concentrate upon the views from the countryside to the town and the views from the town to the countryside. This broad overview is designed to understand town/countryside relationships; therefore, views should be obtained from as many viewpoints as possible, not just from the road.

2. Determine town **entrance points** or **zones of entry** paying special attention to the sequence of entry and how the town unfolds revealing itself and its character. This sequence information should reveal the town's interface with the countryside and locate specific points of arrival within the town.

3. Understand and record the town's **basic structure and organization**. Notice the major streets, intersections, squares, parks, buildings, public places, people's visible activities, significant changes in elevation, special features, vegetation, architecture, discordent or unpleasant images, and new construction.

4. The town's **central area**, unless a very recognizable **special district** is identified, is where the most intensive observation should occur. Special districts may be ones of special homes, a waterfront, nonconcentral new development or similar features. In the central area notice: Public space and how it is being used; buildings and their ability to form outdoor space; landmarks; areas of frequent human activity; and, in general, the organization and perceived edges of the central area. The relationship between buildings and outdoor space is very important; as is the quality of the space and how people are using it.

5. The last item in this organizational framework is to notice and record the town's **details**. Special attention should be paid to the color, form, texture, materials, and construction methods of the objects that bind the town together and produce the myriad of images of particular interest to the pedestrian and other interested observers.[19]

2.21

2.20 A strong sense of enclosure is created by vegetation and the combination of public buildings and commercial structures.

2.21 New functions can occur within older structures without altering essential character ingredients such as architectural style, detail, and human scale.

Organize this material for future presentation, and if required, more detailed analysis. The Team should involve members of the Citizens Advisory Committee in these reconnaissance trips and the resulting dialogue will provide the Team members with the deeper understanding necessary for conducting a meaningful town study.

...EN/TEAM WORKSHOPS

Once this reconnaissance effort of Step Two is ...mpleted, perhaps a period of two or three weeks will be necessary, a series of organized workshops must be conducted by the Team with elected officials, the Citizens Advisory Committee, concerned local citizens, and the manager. Before conducting the workshop, the Team should reflect upon the following suggestions for successfully working with citizens:

1. Never over promise. State what you can do and how you are going to do it: do not promise any more. Gaining the trust and confidence of the town's citizens is important; if this support is ever lost, it can never be regained.

2. Keep the entire process flexible. Do not provide a rigid structure for events; but instead let people participate as equal partners.

3. Gain an understanding for how the people feel about their town and how they use it, and maintain this knowledge as an active ingredient of the study process.

4. Develop a strong, personal rapport with the town's citizens.

5. Make sure the citizens involved represent townwide viewpoints. It is easy for an articulate, minority opinion to result in an imbalance of information or an exclusion of other viewpoints.

6. Have a basic theme and stick to it. Make sure that the entire workshop-participation process centers upon the basic, project objective of town character identification.

7. Allow citizen veto power to exist. Strike a good balance between the Team's professional judgment and the user or citizen's judgment. The major objective of all Phase One workshops is to create a statement which describes the unique aspects or special *spirit of place* possessed by the study town. This should be a balance between the local view and the view ascertained by the Team.

Workshop No. 1 should occur during this first session. During this session the Team will present the results from the initial field studies in the following ways:

1. A verbal statement describing the town's special character.

2. A character map of the town indicating the location of special character places or zones (see Case Study, Chapter Three).

3. A slide, video tape, or movie presentation illustrating the verbal and graphic material.

4. And, most importantly, a statement of the Team's project goals and basic assumptions.

Even though much of the materials presented at this session have been drawn from earlier citizen sessions, the reason for this session is to begin the

2.22

2.23

2.22 *The richness of detail in town environments creates much of a place's image and character.*

2.23 *Local materials often provide much of a place's image. Locating their source is very important to restoration activities which seek to maintain character within new construction.*

2.24

2.25

2.24 Looking into the town provides a keen understanding of its site and physical orientation. The sheep meadow was once the ocean, and the view replicates the original view from approaching ships. (Rye, England)

2.25 This well defined entry is due to the existance of a town wall. Entry points to most towns are less defined; however, their identification is important to understanding town image and structure. (Rye, England)

2.26

2.26 Town character and spirit are often perceived from its streets and ways. This street offers pedestrian scale, handsome materials, and a sense of order and social concern for town quality. (Rye, England)

2.27 The richness of high quality detail permeates the town and is a major contributor to its overall quality and spirit. (Rye, England)

2.27

2.28 The center of town life is indicated by a major square enclosed by principal public and commercial structures. (Rye, England)

process of exposing Team bias to the town's citizens. In this manner they can elicit from the citizens their opinions concerning the presented thoughts and conclusions.

To further facilitate a consensus concerning the workshop objective of creating a basic town character statement and map, the Team should prepare two questionnaires:

1. A comprehensive one to poll the opinions of the Citizen Advisory Committee, the Manager, and the elected officials.

2. A shorter one to be published in the town newspaper for polling the opinions of all citizens. (see Case Study, Chapter Three).

The Team should collect the finished long questionnaires from the Citizens Advisory Committee, and after a reasonable time collect the completed newspaper questionnaires from drop boxes located in various suitable public places such as: City Hall, Post Office, general stores, banks, Police Station, and Sheriff's Office. For conclusions to be valid within the project's overall context, the Team must determine what percentage of agreement is required on any given question. This should be based upon the number of responses and the Team's judgment after evaluating the results. Experience has shown that an agreement of 70-80 percent is sufficient to obtain townwide consensus. Secondary levels of consensus on any given question can also be determined.[20]

Workshop No. 2 using the questionnaire information as a base, the Team should revise the character map to reflect revised values and ideas; and conduct, with the CAC and Manager, a second workshop. This workshop should seek to establish agreement for the map of uniqueness aspects and for a general statement identifying the town's special uniqueness. Activities during this session **might** include:

☐ Slide and movie presentations indicating items mentioned on the questionnaire

☐ Walking tours of the town taken in order to discuss certain aspects of uniqueness while on the specific sites

☐ Discussion and debate concerning the inclusion or deletion of certain areas, or determining if certain areas seem more important than others.

The Team should remember that this map and statement of uniqueness is only an early attempt at mapping the special areas in the town. A much more specific map, resulting from extensive analysis, will be the product of Phase Two. This Phase One map and statement, however, serves an important function in the town study effort. Once the Team's initial research/analysis phase has resulted in the desired product, a statement of town uniqueness, a plateau, has been reached; and the first stage of the Town Uniqueness preservation Plan may be implemented. The work to this point will have been general in nature, having taken just a few weeks, and the graphic showing the town's special areas will be general as well. This level of completeness is desirable in that it can still be flexible, and subject to revision, while at the same time it has enough authority and conviction to be used in the decision-making process.

THE CHARACTER MAP BECOMES A FUNCTIONAL BASE

Assuming that the Team and the Citizens Advisory Committee have reached agreement on PHASE ONE results, a public presentation of the map and its ingredients is made. At this time, barring any major dissension from the public concerning PHASE ONE findings, the Citizens Advisory Committee assumes a new function. Using the PHASE ONE work as a base the Citizens Advisory Committee will become an advisory body to local government. Their role, which becomes adversary as well as advisory, will be to observe general growth and change occurring in the town; and to recommend revision to any proposals for physical change which may be a threat to town character or special sense of place. The advantage of this organized and knowledgeable adversary effort is that as the Team and the Citizens Advisory Committee enter PHASE TWO, which is by its nature time-consuming, with the project's goal of town uniqueness preservation already functioning.

This point in the project can be the end of the town's effort. Should a decision be made that no more planning effort is desired, or affordable, the character map can become an end in itself. If that is the case, the final character map should become the town's official *uniqueness preservation* guide.

The Manager plays a key role at this critical point in the project, that of being a spokesperson for the plan on a daily basis. Despite the plan's evolution based upon townwide participation, it will need to be explained to elected officials, business leaders, citizens groups, and any agencies whose support might be required or desired. This should be the Manager's major responsibility.

To facilitate the Character Map's functioning as the final product the following actions should be taken by elected officials:

1. Create a permanent Citizens Advisory Committee of five to seven persons to monitor town growth and change.

2. Create revolving chairmanships and establish length of service guidelines for the committee.

3. Decide if the project is to continue, or disband the study Team. (Should the decision be made to continue however, the town should proceed with Phase Two. If the recommendation is that the town continue, be certain that enough interest exists to maintain project momentum.)

4. Clearly define the role of the Manager, if one has been hired.

5. Revise the guideline in three years to keep it current.

6. Work in concert with private sector interests to ensure that new development is in harmony with uniqueness preservation goals, and that development guidelines do not unfairly hamper private sector revitalization efforts.

7. Work to place significant buildings, places, or neighborhoods on the state or national register of historic places.

8. Encourage the Citizens Advisory Committee to be active.

PHASE TWO

PHASE TWO of the process consists of Steps Three, Four, and Five and builds upon the base created by PHASE ONE. This PHASE is the heart of the process and requires the most conscientious effort from the Team, the Citizens Advisory Committee, the Manager, and the town's citizens. This PHASE should not begin unless full and complete support for a continued effort exists within town government and among the town's citizens.

The maps of town character created during PHASE ONE located some point specific aspects of town character such as historic buildings, parks, and landmarks as well as limited zones of character such as the river front or old town. While they are a composite of much information they often do not express relative values to any great extent i.e. they do not indicate what is more special than something else. The activity in PHASE TWO is designed to create "A Town Uniqueness Preservation Plan" with levels of priority, to be used for future preservation, enhancement and growth management decisions. These plans will indicate special zones which are based upon relative values, and will identify which areas are the most important.

The major objectives of PHASE TWO, Steps Three, Four and Five are:

☐ To analyze the Natural, Cultural and Visual components of town character and establish values for the ingredients in each heading; thus determining relative values, i.e., what items are more important to town character than others and how they reinforce one another.

☐ To create a series of composite maps which indicate relative levels of uniqueness and identify the important relationship which exists between Natural, Cultural and Visual factors.

☐ To create, with active citizen participation, a plan and a program for the preservation of critical town character or spirit.

2.29 Historical towns which have a distinct spirit of place often result from a sensitivity to site and climate, a strong cultural basis, and the creation of unique visual images.

☐ To establish a mechanism to manage town growth and change as it relates to the preservation of desired town character and quality of life.

Directed by these objectives the Team should conduct the detailed, inventory mapping required to initiate PHASE TWO.

STEP NO. 3 – MAPPING ASPECT

This information should be placed on high quality sepias, polyester film, or photocopied vellums of the townwide base map created in PHASE ONE. These maps must be transparent enough to make overlay composites, using an under-lighted tracing table; and all of the maps must be of the same scale.

A suggestion is to make a town base map for each item to be inventoried and then make a transparent overlay, keyed to that map, of each separate ingredient within the category to be mapped. An example might be topographic slope. If it is mapped in three levels of steepness, 0-5 percent, 5-10 percent, and 10 percent plus; each level of steepness should be put on a separate transparent sheet so that either all levels of slope may be simultaneously overlaid on the base map to reveal the complete topographic pattern or so that any one of the characteristic slope patterns might be studied as it relates to the base map or other character maps. However, if it is determined that only slopes of 10 percent or more create uniqueness, just map those.

This mapping of individual ingredients creates a flexible file system which will allow easy access to data and extensive variation in data manipulation and evaluation. Clear, concise, and consistent symbols should be developed to represent this information. (See appendix page no. 132 for examples.)[21]

NATURE and its activities have placed a signature upon the land and the role these systems

2.30 *The introduction of natural elements such as surface water and vegetation provides much of a place's special quality.*

have played in the creation of town character needs to be understood. Extensive knowledge exists concerning the natural environment, and very sophisticated efforts have been undertaken using nature as the basis for planning and decision making.[22][23] The purpose here, however, is to understand only those basic aspects of the natural environment which most often affect town character. This list can be expanded in any particular town if unique aspects exist which have an obvious impact on quality. The following natural information should be recorded and filed for later use:

1. **Landform** is the basic structure of the natural site. Understanding the process of landform creation (sedimentation, volcanic action, erosion, and glaciation) begins to provide necessary clues to the role of the town's site in creating town character. The general forming process of the town's site should be noted as well as the location of such tangible items as **surface exposed bed rock, ridgelines, and other visible evidences** of landform type.

2. **Topographic relief** mapping will reveal the town's three-dimensional shape, potential or existing points of visual orientation, and knowledge of vegetation and drainage patterns. This mapping will be in levels of elevation, indicated by shading the contour intervals. The interval will vary with the town's steepness and should range from 10-25′. Concurrent with this, a knowledge of **percent of slope**, or levels of steepness, is very useful in understanding existing and future growth suitability. (see Case Study, Chapter 3)

3. **Surface water** is closely related to topography. This mapping activity locates: Watersheds, marsh land, streams, ponds, rivers, lakes and floodplains to obtain a comprehensive understanding of the role water plays as a character component. In cases where land subsidence is present, knowledge of underground water tables and seasonal fluctuations should also be obtained. Also, the availability of water will indicate future growth potential, limitations, and direction.

2.31

2.32

2.31 *Historic structures often enclose public space in older towns. These places produce much of a town's perceived character and should be protected.*

2.32 *Vegetation provides a powerful and unique entry. It should be maintained and replenished as a permanent part of this town's image.*

4. **Soil** types are of particular importance. Note in particular the type of vegetation they will sustain, their erosion susceptibility, and their buildability. Soil reports, consultation, and interpretation are available from the Soil Conservation Service.

5. **Vegetation** is a key indicator of soil and climate; and the interaction of these three elements provides much of the town's image as well as provides knowledge concerning how town growth changes might affect that interaction. Map major stands of vegetation such as woods, forests, grasslands, and riparian growths. **Major trees**, which are located in the public domain and are of 4″ caliper or greater should be identified and mapped. The Team should compile a recommended list of suitable plants for future planting recommendations. The Agricultural Extension Service will provide lists of plants suitable for each county.

6. **Undisturbed natural areas or ecological niches** within a town's fabric often provide important character producers such as open space and seasonal wildlife habitat. These areas should be located very specifically as they are often small in size, and frequently, in private ownership.

7. **Climate** should not be overlooked as it is a key ingredient in understanding vegetation and the potential for outdoor activity. Its various dimensions of seasonal change, rainfall, quantity and clarity of sunlight, and primary direction of wind and air currents will provide valuable information concerning a town's character and mood.

CULTURAL SYSTEMS will include the examination of human interaction with the natural site during the evolution of a town, local cultural attitudes concerning town quality, and people's past and present activities in town. The Team should analyze the following types of information remembering that the goal is to search for cultural aspects which affect town character and not to record the extensive and complicated mass of cultural information which exists:

1. **Historic phases** of town growth, from the existing town plan to the present should be discovered and recorded. Special attention should be paid to the edges of each growth phase; it is often there that significant juxtapositions occur. Historic buildings and districts which may already be established, based upon state or national criteria, should also be recorded on maps.

2. **Existing public and quasi-public infrastructure** such as schools, day care centers, community centers, parks, open space, sidewalks, cemeteries, churchs, police stations, fire stations, and utility systems must be located and represented on a map. Determine the full range of places in the public or quasi-public domain and what role they serve in producing town

image. These areas often do not change frequently and thus can become the backbone of a character preservation and enhancement program.

3. **Existing zoning and land use** mapping will lend understanding to how the town is being used and the full range of legislative and administrative controls being used or which are available. Locate trends and conflicts between zoning and land use.

4. **New development proposals** both public and private should be noted. Often this information is difficult to acquire. However, it is critical to the identification of potential impact upon town character. Ask developers, bankers, real estate brokers; and listen for rumors.

5. **Town organization, structure, and shape** should be determined using the "path, node, edge, landmark, and district" classification system or some reorganization and redefinition more suitable to the study area.[24] This investigation should include a thorough understanding of the transportation network, key public gathering spaces, identifiable districts, social enclaves, townspeople's image and knowledge of their town, and what the townspeople's sentiments are with regards to their mental town image. In particular, locate the entrances, points of arrival, major routes, major structures, and major activity places. This is more specific and detailed continuation of work undertaken in PHASE ONE. The following examples indicate the types of town structure the Team is likely to encounter. It is important that the Team be aware of the various advantages and disadvantages each offers and the role they play in creating character.

☐ *The grid* is the most common town shape encountered in American towns. This form was introduced early in the settlement of America and is encountered in every state. Its many advantages include: Its ability to adapt to large and complex scales; its simple and convenient orientation; the ease with which circulation may be directed to certain lines of the grid; and its expansion flexibility. One major disadvantage is monotony; however,

2.33 New development proposals for selected town parts can have a positive affect upon town image, while allowing needed economic revitalization and development to occur.

TOWN SHAPE

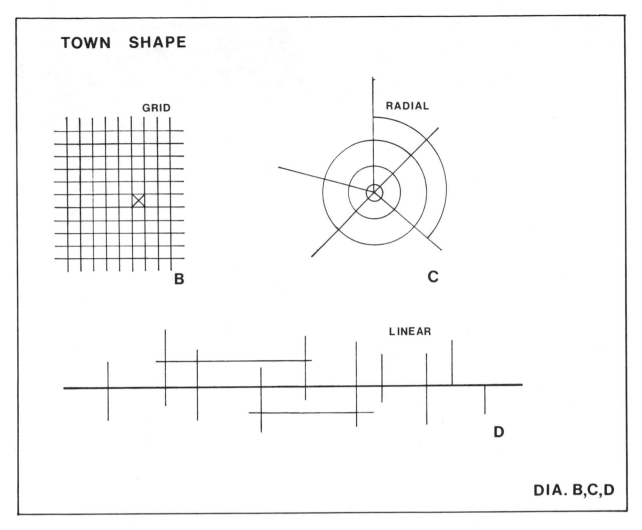

GRID

RADIAL

B

C

LINEAR

D

DIA. B,C,D

such variation as topography or grid modifications such as wider streets, diagonal connections, and superimposed rings can overcome this aspect. (See Diagram B)

☐ *Radial towns* are less common; however, the popular use of ringroads and loop by-pass systems has reorganized many towns to this pattern. Some advantages are: The ability to add rings or loops to allow various by-passing routes in conjunction with central flow; the potential for branching and/or connection to sub-centers; and the ease of orientation. Disadvantages include: Traffic concentration at the center; lack of the flexibility offered by the grid; and the radial is not easily converted to non-central flow. (See Diagram C)

☐ *Linear configuration*, such as along a main highway that parallels the railroad, is seen in many small towns. This form often has many cross streets and few streets parallel to the main highway; directs movement from one point to another; is economical in its use of materials; and cross streets may be designed to allow intersections and utilities to be easily organized for efficiency now and ease of

connection later for future growth. Problems that exist are the lack of focus or center and the potential to become congested with entry and exit traffic at cross streets, curb cuts, and private driveways. (See Diagram D)

6. **Activities** such as how people actually use the town is often as important as the physical aspects we have just been discussing. These human activities within the town go beyond "land use" and include the myriad of interconnected happenings that provide town life and excitement. Unfortunately, these activities are often the unseen casualty of growth and change; and their loss or disruption can drain the vitality of a town or districts with a town. The Team must understand these activities and the role they play in the formation of town character. Keeping in mind the character identification focus of these investigations, the Team should look at how a typical day or week is organized by the various town's citizens. A suggested method is to look at activity in terms of "behavior streams;" the overall categories of activities such as recreation, work, shopping, housework, and child care; and the detailed activities within these overall activities. For example recreation might be a game of catch, bike riding, fishing, walking, or

lunch in a cafe. Each of these activities will have its own character producing elements, and a setting in which it is most appropriate.[25] Questionnaires alone will not provide this important information, and such aids as observation and interviews with citizens will be required to gain full understanding.[26] A suggestion is to gain detailed information from the Citizens Advisory Committee concerning their activies; and if the mix of the Committee is good, a fairly accurate picture of town activities should emerge. Other items to be aware of, and recorded, include:

□ *Unique or seasonal activities* such as fairs, festivals, annual contests, parades, rodeos, tournaments, and other scheduled events. Note where in town they happen and when. These activities are frequently major image producers and also may draw many outsiders to town.

□ *Potential learning experiences* offered by the natural or cultural environment such as music events, local crafts, geologic, horitcultural or agricultural uniqueness.

□ *Major activity spots* should be located and noted whether or not the place reflects the activity.

□ *Unique or special recreational habits* such as "cruising" or "hanging out" which are important and would be easy to disrupt if not understood.

□ *Special activities or holidays within neighborhoods or ethnic enclaves* should be noted and respected, for much of the character of a town comes from these ethnic groups.

7. **"Public"** areas which are not in public ownership should be reviewed as they might have been indicated on the "Public Areas" information of the Infrastructure Map. These areas, such as vacant lots and stream banks, are often heavily used for recreation; and their potential for public ownership should be investigated. Much of a town's character is perceived from its public area and the majority of recommendations made in PHASE TWO of this report will relate to those areas. Therefore, the Team should determine what areas people think of as private and public, how they feel about public areas, and how much freedom to move about exists in the town. This information will be extremely helpful in determining the levels of support the Team might expect for public area improvements. This information, to the extent it is possible, should be mapped to the same scale and level of detail as all previous information. (See Case Study, Chapter Three)

2.34

2.35

2.34 *Seasonal activities such as art festivals, craft fairs, rodeos, and regional cook-offs provide much of a place's character. Understanding how, where, and when they occur is very important.*

2.35 *Unique image is often created by strong visual landmarks.*

2.36

2.37

2.36 Creation of functions which produce activity is very important to town revitalization.

2.37 The restoration of unique town elements, in this case a historic canal revitalized as a pedestrian walkway, should be the goal of town parts analysis and design.

VISUAL SYSTEMS and **TOWN APPEARANCE** comprehension is the next aspect of mapping in this Step. These items are the result of human interaction with the landscape, and it is frequently the visual perception of a place which establishes its image or character. Appearance evaluation is difficult, often subjective, and hard to adequately quantify to the extent that general public agreement is possible. The following material, however, will provide the necessary data to create a successful visual appearance component at the townwide scale. The information gained from these investigations is ofttimes overlapping; however, the congruence of zones or specific points within the categories add value, as congruence gives authority to appearance conclusions and facilitates general agreement. An example would be the occurrence of several appearance components in one small area.

Appearance components should be assessed and mapped with extensive photos keyed to the mapped areas. These components consist of the following:

☐ *Views into and out of the town* which seek to obtain comprehensive understanding of the town's visual form as one moves through and around it.

☐ *Visual orientation features* such as landmarks, water, points of visual overlook, skylines, and building profiles.

☐ Assessment of *sense of place* and *areas of unified visual character* or *areas where sense of place is disrupted*.

☐ *Pedestrian life* and its quality implications; noting such things as movement, viewpoints, how the time of day or year affects sense of place, complexity, and visual access to areas of interest.

☐ *Entrance points and gateways*, the relationship between physical and visual sense of arrival, should be located. Does the transition from one district to another have a discrete visual expression?

☐ Indications of the *preservation of unique areas,* scenic or historic features and buildings should be noted. Has the town attempted preservation, and do the results have a visual impact on town image?

☐ The location of *buildings or structures* which are important to town image, even though they are not particularly historic such as a hilltop structure which catches the full glow of morning light.

☐ Assess the town's particular *spatial definitions*, enclosure and sequence at the town scale, such as the relationship of valley/ridge enclosure, major street enclosures, or proportion and height of buildings to open space. Much of this information should be available from PHASE ONE's initial town inventory.

2.38 *Views from a town's public spaces should be maintained and their importance to overall town spirit should be understood.*

2.39 *Neglect can damage character; however, the opportunity for revitalization and the potential for positive change is still available despite the existing neglect.*

☐ *Perceived positive and negative aspects of town appearance* should be identified. Obtain visual examples of these aspects.

☐ Visual clues of *the passage of time*, both seasonal and historic, should be noted.[27]

☐ The presence of *amenities* and *uglies*, the good and bad image producers, should be recorded. Note the difference between required uglies like scrap heaps, auto junkyards, coal heaps, utility stations, and unnecessary uglies such as billboards, fastfood ("logo") architecture, and treeless parking lots.

☐ Note the affect of *non-visual sensory factors*, such as noise, smell, taste, and touch, upon town quality.

☐ Locate the *visual edges of the various ranges of vision* of near range, middle range, and far range. Determine at what point of range is the view stopped or interrupted from various key viewing spots. Note the change of perceived town scale due to these edges.

☐ *Details*, the myriad little objects existing in the visual spectrum, should be inventoried. These objects create the visual complexity which can

2.39

2.40

2.41

2.40 *Historical artifacts provide a link to a place's past and should be preserved as part of overall town image.*

2.41 *Rich architectural detail can provide outstanding image. If an entire street or neighborhood has similar image, it will become a major uniqueness area.*

give a town its special charater and *spirit of place*. Note such items as doorways, cornice lines, lighting details, grill work, personalized signs, and miscellaneous street hardware.

☐ Consider the visual role of *plant materials* and how they affect town form. Seasonal change is a key factor.

☐ Assess the *impact of change* on the visual environment, and the visual environment's ability to absorb change while retaining character.

☐ Indicate the *opportunities for improvement*, given the best of all possible worlds and the known constraints, without destroying character. Are there potential vistas that could be opened or poor views altered?

☐ Note the *point specific appearance components*. Refer to the photographic examples provided here and note such items as:

- *Panorama points* and what is seen from them, and what the view means to the viewer

- *Vistas*, with particular emphasis upon what terminates them, i.e. buildings, open space, distant hills, etc.

- *A glimpse* to an important object or view

- *Potential views* which may be developed

- *Unpleasant specific views*, as defined by the town's citizens or the Team responding to citizen values

- *Focal points*, major or minor objects which terminate vistas

- *Views to open space*, both public and private

- *Views to water*, in all of its visual aspects

- *Special streets*, as identified from questionnaires, the identification of common elements on those streets

- *Symbols* which may have meaning beyond their visual images, i.e. memorials, statues, abandoned mill buildings, and railroad depots[29,29]

Once this structured viewing has occurred the Team must glean from this guideline list, and their observations, those items of **importance to visual uniqueness within the specific study town.** The symbols indicating these items must then be displayed upon maps which are compatible in scale with the "Natural" and "Cultural" information. This scale consistency will be very critical in the creation of the Town Uniqueness Preservation map which is the all important end product of this PHASE.

The final Visual composite map will indicate zones of visual uniqueness based upon the congruence of visual appearance components within given areas of the town. This map should be in levels compatible with the uniqueness levels previously found for the Natural and Cultural uniqueness composite maps.

2.42

2.43

2.44

2.42 Seasonal change and vegetation are an important aspect of a region's visual quality.

2.43 A successful technique for creating pedestrian space in special districts is the use of temporary barricades. This action satisfies the pedestrian need for auto-free space and allows for the opening up of views and vistas from the street.

2.44 Cultural expressions, such as this courthouse which terminates a vista, provide many of a town's unique visual aspects.

2.45 Views to activity and scenic objects should be maintained as part of any Uniqueness Preservation Plan.

2.45

2.46

2.47

2.46 Town parks and commons provide a positive image. As change occurs, they may need revision to meet new needs; however, this revision should always maintain the original spirit of place.

2.47 Unique town image is often a product of building groupings, materials, orientation, and the quality of light. This view from the town beach helps establish the character of that important town part.

To obtain the composite, overlay the various maps of appearance components which were created; and note those zones which contain the most indication of special visual uniqueness. Determine which zones are the most important, and establish the Visual composite map in two or three levels. (See Case Study, Chapter Three) Augment these conclusions with the information gained from the following suggestion and develop the final Visual Composite Map.

Conversations with the Citizens Advisory Committee, including the Manager, regarding their detailed thoughts about the visual aspects of the town, should occur concurrently with the mapping activities. The Team should ask each member to mark up maps indicating their thoughts concerning the town's special visual aspects. These maps should then be correlated with Team mapping efforts, and the areas of agreement between the Team and citizens should be noted. This exercise should result in a map or a series of maps which accurately depict the significant visual aspects of the town. Experience has indicated that when the values of the local citizens are used to obtain visual information their support for aesthetics as a factor in decision making is very strong.[30] A key judgment ingredient, based upon citizen opinion, is congruence. An example of this being: If most people think a certain street is visually unique, it most likely will be.

It is very important that the Team and the citizens understand that these visual factors are as critical to a town's uniqueness as natural and cultural information. While much overlap occurs between what is called visual, as opposed to natural and cultural; it is often the seen result of the natural-cultural interaction which creates uniqueness. Therefore, it is most important that this visual analysis convert that interaction into pure visual terms which have values similar to the natural and cultural ingredients.

TOWN PARTS are those areas or places within the town fabric that are identified as special during the townwide appraisals. Many of these places often become design focus areas in PHASE THREE; and will require a more detailed analysis before actual design studies are undertaken. Some of this effort will overlap previous analysis; however, the analysis is conducted in much more detail. Areas often located and investigated during this activity include: Town squares; "Main Street" downtown; a commons or central park; waterfronts; historic districts and neighborhoods; and crossroads. This analysis should concern itself with the public space which exists in these areas, the buildings that define or enclose the space (including a detailed analysis of building facades fronting on the area) and the linkage elements which connect the area to other areas. These spaces are often the memorable spots or distinct places which can make a town unique and unforgettable.

It should be noted that this analysis of town parts will not be used to create the town uniqueness plan which is the intended product of PHASE TWO of the proposed process. This information is critical in the design and revitalization of selected parts of the town, however, and should become part of the overall town data base. While this task could wait and be undertaken in PHASE THREE, experience has shown that it is more efficiently done as part of the broader based analytical tasks.

The basic notion behind this effort is drawn from various published works which speak directly to this issue. This background material is provided to establish the base level of understanding the Team should have before conducting this important step. In his landmark studies of European town parts, Camillo Sitte stated that his central idea was "to investigate a multitude of fine old squares and other urban arrangements with a view to finding the **reasons** for the **fine effects**, because the reasons, recognized rightly, would then represent a sum of rules which, when followed, would lead to comparable excellent effects."[31] The important aspect of this statement was Sitte's realization that certain towns and town parts had special character and that with careful study the character or effect could be understood, as well as could the **reasons** behind the effects. His search for design rules which would allow these places to be reproduced elsewhere however has been seriously questioned as a desirable and useful concept. Speaking to this issue Edward Sekler suggested that, "one will no longer share without qualification the optimism of Sitte, yet there is a profound truth when he speaks of the **reasons** and not of the **effects** alone." Expanding upon the need to understand the reasons and not just the effects Sekler says, "Something of direct formal applicability an **effect**, cannot be derived from historic examples in urban design. Every attempt in this direction is doomed to failure because it negates urban form (in our case town parts) as something which has its full reality in the unique context of its creation, and in the uniqueness of its existence. We are not dealing with mental abstractions that can be reproduced at will, such as the symbols of logic and mathematics, but with sensual realities which came into existence under conditions that cannot be repeated and which exist in a unique perceptible connection from which they cannot be separated without becoming something different."[32] In this case the team should look at the town's parts for the reasons why a particular town part is unique and special. This analysis seeks to discover these reasons so that meaningful and proper design decisions for these areas might be made during preservation and revitalization activities. This task is designed to produce the information required to prevent the often ruinous results of "improvements" to key public areas. The way to avoid this problem is to understand the context, in this case the town. Then to understand its special parts in greater detail; not just themselves, but their relationship to each other, to

2.48

2.49

2.48 A first impression shows that historic structures, even with modest renovation, can remain a viable part of a place's economy and special image.

2.49 Neglected railroad areas should be improved as they may become important town places when changing transportation trends play a more active role in town life.

46

2.50

2.51

2.50 *Views to visual landmarks provide much of a town's special character. The disruption of these views will erode the spirit of place created by the enclosure of open space.*

2.51 *Historic street names can evoke meaning and establish a sense of place which is often stronger than that created by architectural style or landscape. They often indicate how a place was used in the past or how old functions might still remain.*

the town as a whole, and their relative quality based upon comparative analysis.

A suggested organizational format for these more detailed studies (in particular: streets, spaces, enclaves, or special districts) consists of a series of suggested work tasks. These more detailed analytical tasks should proceed in a similar manner to the townwide analysis previously undertaken. Base maps should be created which indicate the town part to be analyzed, at a suitable scale to record detail, and reproduced in multiple copies. The information obtained should then be displayed on the maps, using suitable headings, and augmented with sketches, diagrams, photos, and text. Compile the information into mini-reports for each place so that they will be useful in determining the role these places play in overall town uniqueness expression. An additional role is their potential use as background data for specific design projects which may be undertaken at some future time, perhaps in a PHASE THREE option. The recommended tasks are as follows:[33]

1. **First impression** should be captured, by the Team of the place under active investigation. As a response to this visual image is obtained, the Team should attempt to understand why the place generates the image that it does; and begin to ask what its special qualities are.

   Careful documentation of the visual image, using photographs, video tapes, or sketches of the place should also be undertaken during this and other initial visits. The process of obtaining this information varies and such tasks as walking around the area, conducting "windshield surveys," reviewing air photos, and talking to people often are employed. Another skill that might be practiced is the fine art of setting and obtaining information by personal observation.[34]

2. **Time** is the next area of analytical concern. An understanding of how a place physically evolved over time may provide useful information concerning potential future evolution or the potential impact of change. Old photographs, newspaper accounts, and interviews with long time residents can provide much information during this important activity.

   Attempt to understand how the area or place became special; what events over time contributed to its uniqueness; and ask, if at some time, was it better? or is it as good today as it ever was? Answers to these questions will provide important design clues should decisions need to be made concerning the alteration of these places.

3. **Scale** is the third issue with which the Team should be concerned. This extremely important aspect of scale should increase the understanding of the physical being of the place, space, or area undergoing detailed analysis. It is this step in the town parts analysis where the

quality of the space, its enclosing or defining elements, and its various linkages must be completely understood. The measure during this activity should be the human figure and how it relates to such elements as:

☐ *Building heights, and the space buildings and trees might enclose* – The mechanics of human vision provide some clues on how to determine the amount of enclosure which occurs in an outdoor space or street. A person sees 60-75 degrees to the left and right of center for a cone of vision approximately 120-150 degrees. At eye-level-vision a person sees 30 degrees above eye level and 45 degrees below eye level.[35] Therefore, four approximate levels of enclosure might be said to occur:

(1) Full enclosure occurs when a facade height equals the distance we stand from a building (a 1:1 or greater proportion) in which case the cornice (or upper line of the form) is at an angle of 45 or more degrees from the line of horizontal sight. Because this is of a greater angle than the 30 degree maximum of upper level forward vision a person feels enclosed. Enclosures of less than 1:1 will become increasingly confining and less comfortable.

(2) *Less than full* enclosure occurs when a facade height equals one-half of the distance we stand from a building, a proportion of 1:2. This is a 30 degree angle of vision and provides enclosure at the threshold of perceived enclosure and distraction.

SPACES WHICH DO NOT ENCLOSE THE VIEWER:

(3) *Minimum enclosure* is found to happen when the proportion equals 1:3, the enclosing elements are seen at an 18 degree angle, and objects beyond the facades are a part of the scene.

(4) *Loss of enclosure*, and often the loss of sense of place, happens when the facade height is one-fourth the distance from the facade, a 1:4 proportion, thus allowing the viewer to see the cornice at a fourteen degree angle when more than half of the view is of beyond the space. (See Diagram E, page 49) It is important to remember that people move around and that these angles and dimensions are just guidelines for understanding the relative enclosure qualities of a place like a courthouse square.[36]

☐ *The shape of the area or space* – Most public spaces will be squares, rectangles, circles, "L" shapes, triangles, or some combination of these forms. Other, less common, types of spatial shapes to evaluate might include: A

2.52

2.53

2.52 Human scale and function are very important to the study and revision of special town parts.

2.53 The strong sense of place. encountered in many European plazas is often lacking in American small towns. However, ingredients such as enclosure, human scale, activities, and changing functions are always present and should be incorporated into preservation and revitalization plans.

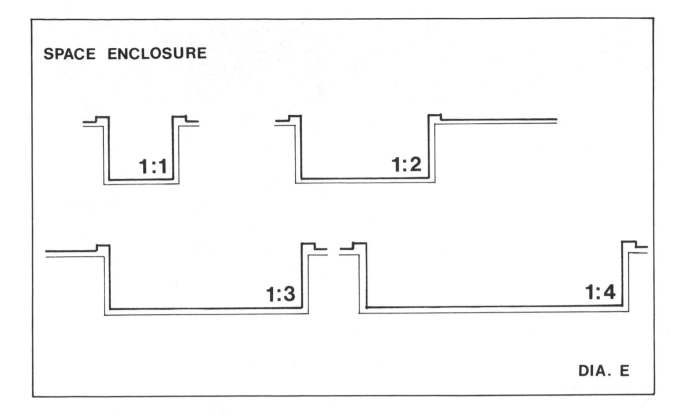

SPACE ENCLOSURE

1:1

1:2

1:3

1:4

DIA. E

channel, like a street or riverfront, enclosed on two sides; an area that is defined but lacking any enclosing elements, like a large town commons or plaza; or a place which is dominated by a building and having minor enclosing elements, like a structure centered in a large plaza. Each of these variations, including the more common shapes, must be analyzed to suit the particular situation.

☐ *The linkage systems* – The "transitions" between parts such as steps, ramps, walks, arcades, and streets play an important role in the perceived character of a place.

☐ *Building facades* – The parts being studied will have enclosing elements such as buildings, walls, trees, ground forms, or water. One important aspect of this analysis should be the building facades, their image, overall condition, color and texture, potential for preservation or revitalization, and importance to town character. This information is best displayed on drawings, which can be produced from photographs or on boards of mounted photographs which are assembled into a montage, of the entire street facade.

☐ *Specific visual ingredients and effects* – The major value of such an inventory is the ability to locate this information spatially on town parts maps and therefore draw conclusions as to **visual complexity** and **interest** of a place based upon congruence, or clustering of these ingredients. The basis for much of these suggestions was developed by the

Townscape Movement in England; however, the variations of time and geographic place often necessitate alterations which reflect, to a greater extent, the specific study area. This investigation should be conducted in very fine grained detail and might include the following headings:

(1) **Place** includes the visual impacts of such items as vistas, outdoor rooms, and focal points.

(2) **Content** includes ideas like juxtaposition, relationships, intricacy, and netting.

(3) **Details** investigates the visual effect of items such as steps, lighting, plants, texture, and paving.

To undertake this level of analysis, the study Team must have a good working knowledge of the original source material, or similar material.[37]

4. **Function**, how people actually use the place, must be understood. The Team should determine what activities happen there, and when they happen. The Team must also ask: How could the place be better done; are there problems with the original organization or design; does its current function serve current social needs; and can new programs be imposed without disruption of its special qualities. The answers to these and similar questions will begin to establish a series of program constraints which will establish the potential for constructive change or the need for creative preservation. The special town parts are often settings for various

49

2.54

2.55

50

2.56

2.57

2.54 High quality building facades, and their proper restoration, produce much of a town's special image.

2.55 Traditional materials are often used to create a link between existing town image and new functions required by revitalization. The use of cobble paving, consistent planting and street furniture provide a continuity between old and new.

2.56 Modest structures often have a history and function which can not be understood by appearance alone. This commercial establishment plays a major social role as a gathering place and town focal point.

2.57 Activities such as street vendors, musicians, and artists give special quality to public space. They should be maintained or encouraged as part of a town's uniqueness preservation program.

types of behavior and often play a major role within the town. The Team should record such items as:

☐ *Where people enter* the area most frequently.

☐ What *types of activities* happen in the buildings which define the place. Notice which ones are generators of human activity (such as bars, cafes, or post offices) or those less busy ones (like non-public oriented office space).

☐ Understand how *the time of day* and perhaps *the season of the year* affects how the place is used.

☐ *What people like to do in the place*, given less restrictions or constraints.

☐ Any *special events* which might happen there such as outdoor fairs, markets, or parades.

☐ *What changes might improve the place* without disruption of significant existing cultural patterns.

☐ *New activities which might increase activitiy* and improve economic vitality. This is a key point as many of these places have potential to be better given sound economic as well as physical change.

This list can be quite long and as specific as time and resources permit. The major point is to record and understand the basic activities and functions of the town part being studied so that suggestions for preservation or change might be made without creating disharmony among the users or potential users.

**STEP FOUR –
SYNTHESIS: CREATING THE COMPOSITES AND PLAN**

Once the analysis portion of PHASE TWO is complete this information becomes the basis for the creation of a townwide uniqueness preservation plan which will establish the guidelines for town preservation and revitalization activities. As the entire process re-cycles, part of the data which has been collected must be revised and in some cases new or more detailed data must be obtained. The desire should be, however, to minimize the collection of data to only that which is required to obtain the desired results of PHASE TWO.

STEP FOUR is one of creative synthesis. It will bring together in a logical way all of the data, including citizen values, which has been collected and analyzed in previous project steps. During the early part of this step the Study Team, the Citizens Advisory Committee, and the Manager should conduct a new series of meetings and workshops with town citizens. These sessions should be designed to execute the final listing of town goals and to identify the final ingredients of town uniqueness which occur within the Natural, Cultural, and Visual realms. Using the data maps

2.58 *The creation of pedestrian districts as part of downtown revitalization efforts adds activity and improves the quality of life. To work well these districts must be part of an overall town plan for circulation, parking, and economic incentives.*

which are stored in the inventory and analysis file system, the Team should proceed to create the Town Uniqueness Preservation Plan. At this point it should be assumed that enough understanding of the town exists to create a plan which represents the town's Genius Loci and *spirit of place*; and that the values which created the understanding have been based upon complete majority consensus. The development of this consensus is of extreme importance before the technical process of plan emergence begins; as this consensus value system will serve as the basis for future efforts. The basic task of this step is to identify and put a value upon each ingredient which has been noted as important during the analysis activities. For example, if it is agreed that a certain natural ingredient, such as evergreen vegetation, is critical to town image; it may be given twice as much value, in the creation of the natural composite, as the presence of surface bedrock.

Once these values and relative weightings have been established for each aspect of Natural, Cultural and Visual information, the technical process of creating composites can begin. The actual process of creating the composites and plan

is indicated by Diagram F (page 53). This activity should be conducted in the following manner:

1. **A composite map of town uniqueness ingredients** for each category of Natural, Cultural and Visual should be created by the Team by drawing from the mapped inventory materials. The composites should be in two or three levels of uniqueness value and the number of values should be *consistent* with each of the three categories; i.e., if the Natural composite is in two levels of value, the Cultural and Visual composite must also have only two levels. These maps are created from the data file by simultaneously overlaying each selected Natural element. Use either the complete map or the overlay which shows just one ingredient, chosen as being special based upon Team consensus, on a light table until a pattern of those most important areas begin to emerge. This pattern will be based upon the congruence of uniqueness ingredients. As each overlay indicating an area of special features is superimposed, the zones of congruence (areas which contain more than one value) will begin to appear as a darker image. The darkest zone, based upon greatest concentration

of values, will be the most important to protect for town uniqueness preservation. These zones will be flexible and the Teams judgement must be used to establish the precise zones which will appear on the final composite map. This judgement will be reinforced by the Team's knowledge of townspeople's values.

Once this pattern emerges, it should be recorded upon a separate map (See Case Study, Chapter Three) which indicates two or three levels of uniqueness value. The end result of this process will be three composite maps which indicate the most unique area within the realm of the three categories: Natural, Cultural, and Visual. It is very important to keep these categories separate until this point. Were they to be combined too early a change in one category's basic data would change the entire final composite. Keeping this separation allows for last minute or future changes in the individual composites without requiring frequent changes in the final Town Uniqueness Preservation Plan.

2. When the composites have been created and agreement that they represent an accurate portrayal of each category's uniqueness values, the final Town Uniqueness Preservation Plan can be produced. The creation of this final composite produces the end result of PHASE TWO, the *Town Uniqueness Preservation Plan.* (See Case Study, Chapter Three)

Using the direct overlay process, the three composites are super-imposed and the darker areas in the resulting pattern will indicate areas of high uniqueness value which need preservation and sensitive revitalization. While this map could produce many levels of value, it should be restricted to two or three levels for its

final form. Such restructuring helps reduce categories and creates a much simpler plan. This plan is the **heart of the process**, the **major objective of the process**, and shall be the **basis for all future town preservation and revitalization** decision making.

PLAN GUIDELINES

The *Town Uniqueness Preservation Plan* will consist of two or three zones which are considered to have value for preservation of town character. The ingredients which designated these zones are the aspects of the town which the Team and the Citizen's Advisory Committee determined created the town's *Genius Loci*, or, *spirit of place.*

As a final step in plan creation the Team should write General Development Guidelines for each level of town uniqueness which is indicated on the plan. These Guidelines will provide the basis for future judgments concerning growth and change in the uniqueness zones. These Guidelines should state in very simple terms what types of change might occur without damage to a zone's uniqueness values. They should not only speak to land use, but should also speak to the height, bulk, color, scale, materials, texture, and image of new development. The Guidelines should also address such issues as: planting, signs and graphics, lighting, utilities, parking areas and building orientation. Each Team and Committee will need to decide the required level of Guideline detail. However, the Guidelines should be kept general and allow for some flexibility during the town's evolution.

The Plan, if properly conceived, will indicate those areas within the town which give it its special character, spirit, and image: The Genius Loci.

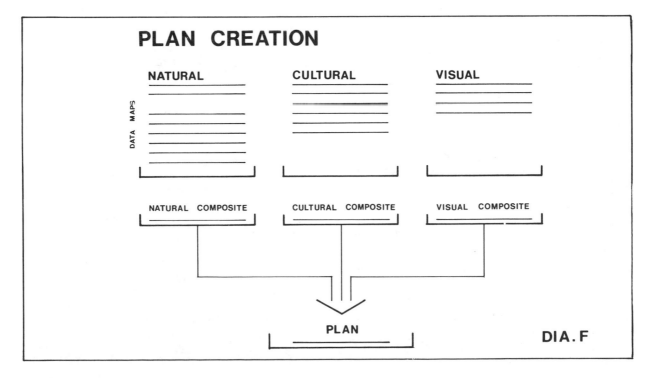

STEP FIVE –
USING THE PLAN

Two major roles are played by the Plan, and both of them require the creation of the plan's companion component, the Town Uniqueness Preservation Committee. This committee should be made up of a representative cross section of townspeople who were active in the plan's evolution, understand the Town Uniqueness Preservation Plan, and are willing to work to see it realized. This is the end of the original Citizen Advisory Committee, and the point at which the Manager can provide the leadership suggested for that role. In creating this new committee each town should clearly define such items as: Individual length of service, process for election to the committee, specific duties, and compensation. These items will vary with each individual situation. Another option is that the town may also elect to retain the original Citizen Advisory Committee as the new Town Uniqueness Preservation Committee, or at least retain some of the members on the new committee.

A suggested group of duties, activities, and powers is provided here to serve as an organizational guide for the function of the new committee:

1. The Committee should have **review power** over all proposed growth and change proposals within the area covered by the *Town Uniqueness Preservation Plan*. This includes private proposals as well as Town, County, State or Federal proposals. Any proposals coming before the Committee would be evaluated against the Town Uniqueness Preservation Plan, and recommendations would then be made to town leaders as to the suitability of the proposal. This evaluation will identify any conflicts between the development and the Plan, provide suggested revisions to the proposal, and become a component in final implementation decisions. The most important function of the *Town Uniqueness Preservation Plan* and the Town Uniqueness Preservation Committee occurs at this point of dealing with evaluation and recommendation. This activity is directly related to the goals and values drawn from the entire planning and design process and should include the tasks which follow.

2. The Committee should work closely with planning agencies and other concerned citizen groups helping to coordinate all efforts on the town's behalf.

3. The Committee should continually reevaluate town goals and the values that went into the *Town Uniqueness Preservation Plan*. These goals must not become dogmatic. They must, however, be kept flexible if these plans are to become living, working documents reflective of the broad based, citizen participation which

resulted as part of the process of evolving these goals.

4. The Committee should hold workshops with potential, private sector developers on a regular basis to inform them of the plan's goals and explore development opportunities within the context of the Plan goals and sound economics.

5. The Committee should be given the power to conduct special studies and to suggest revisions to the *Town Uniqueness Preservation Plan,* based upon changing values, new circumstances, economic conditions, and new technology.

Once the Committee is formed the *Town Uniqueness Preservation Plan* can begin its function of town preservation and enhancement. To facilitate this function the town must enact legislation supporting the *Uniqueness Plan* and making it the official town policy for those areas included in the Plan. Once the *Town Uniqueness Preservation Plan* is official, it can guide development in the unique areas by serving as the legal frame of reference within which the Committee judges development proposals. When a development proposal comes before the Committee for inclusion in the town uniqueness zone, its impact upon the ingredients making up that zone will be determined; and the Committee should make one of the following recommendations:

1. **YES –** The development is not in violation of town uniqueness preservation policies and should be encouraged.

2. **NO –** Revisions must be made to bring the development into line with town policy and the project may be resubmitted for approval.

3. **NO –** Choose an alternative site within the uniqueness zone; and, if required, modify development to match town policy.

4. **NO –** Choose an alternate use for the site. Proposed use is not appropriate for the town uniqueness zone.

A critical aspect of this process is that the person requesting development must have been given full access to the rationale behind the *Town Uniqueness Preservation Plan*, the town ingredients upon which value has been placed, town policy vis-a-vis development within the uniqueness zone, and a right to appeal the decision made by the Town Uniqueness Preservation Committee. The recommendation of the committee must never be arbitrary or capricious, but rather be based upon a public set of guidelines drawn from the *Town Uniqueness Preservation Plan.*

The guidelines for the Committee may be general, or very specific: it will depend upon each town and how it views the role of the Committee. As with the entire process, the goal of these policies should be to protect **town uniqueness** while allowing for needed **growth, change,** and **private sector development.** PHASE TWO of the suggested process ends at this point with the successful completion of the *Town Uniqueness Preservation Plan* and the organization of the Town Uniqueness Preservation Committee. Part and parcel to these two functions are the development policies, within the town uniqueness zones, which were established by the Team and the Citizen Advisory Committee and are based upon the results of the process outlined in this book. This plan is not, however, an end-state document; but can, and should, be monitored and updated as its policies are implemented, and the results evaluated. The Town Uniqueness Plan Committee and the Town should always ask the following questions:

1. Do the results measure up to our expectations?

2. Are the results in keeping with the dual objectives of "uniqueness preservation" and "citizen participation?"

3. What alterations can be made to improve the results?

4. Is the whole system of plans, committees, citizen involvement, managers, special projects, and option selection working? If not, what revisions and changes can be made?

PHASE THREE –
OPTIONS BEYOND THE TOWN UNIQUENESS PLAN

The activities which occur beyond the formation of the *Town Uniqueness Preservation Plan* and the creation of the Town Uniqueness Preservation Committee will vary with each town. At this point the Team which has created the plan should have been disbanded; and the Committee and, hopefully, a Manager should be actively using the Plan to guide town uniqueness preservation.

Each town must now decide if it should pursue additional planning activities; or if the Plan which has just been completed is adequate for current and future needs. The following options may provide guidance during this decision making process:

I. OPTION ONE –
THE COMPREHENSIVE PLAN

Many towns undertaking the uniqueness preservation process do not have comprehensive plans or zoning ordinances. A future role which the *Town Uniqueness Preservation Plan* can play is by serving as a base from which to undertake such efforts and by acting as a temporary plan until such comprehensive planning efforts can be completed. The most important role the *Town Uniqueness Preservation Plan* can play in a comprehensive plan's formulation or revision, is to become an equal part of that plan. The inclusion of the often

neglected aspects of uniqueness and character preservation into the comprehensive plan component will avoid plans which propose growth and change without respect to a town's Genius Loci. This will allow the *Town Uniqueness Preservation Plan* to become equal to the traditional components of comprehensive plans: Transportation, housing, utilities, industrial, open space, health care, parks and recreation, and economic development. In this manner the total range of environmental issues will be examined before a comprehensive plan is formulated and the **quality aspects**, the ones often overlooked or poorly considered, will enter equally into plans and policies.

If the creation or revision of a comprehensive plan and zoning ordinance is the chosen route; all future implementation, monitoring, evaluation, updating, master planning, and special projects design should occur under the auspices of that comprehensive plan. The Town Uniqueness Preservation Committee should continue to function and should retain its role of reviewing any proposed change or impact upon the zones identified for preservation. In this situation where a town has chosen to undertake a comprehensive plan, the following four additional options should be incorporated into the functions of the Plan and the planning staff. Still functioning, however, will be the Manager and the Town Uniqueness Preservation Committee. Their role will be to monitor the *Town Uniqueness Preservation Plan* in the manner described in PHASE TWO, and to ensure that the values relating to town uniqueness preservation are always included in comprehensive plan decision making. If, however, a town elects to not undertake a comprehensive plan, the Manager and Committee can select from the following options those activities they determine to be most beneficial to town uniqueness preservation.

II. OPTION TWO –
A PUBLIC SPACE PLAN

This option concentrates upon the creation of a *Townwide Public Space Plan*, which is created by the incorporation of town uniqueness aspects into a townwide structure.

"Public space" is used here to mean those areas within the town fabric which are open and accessible to the public, both visually and physically. This space, which is open to the freely chosen and spontaneous actions of people, includes such aspects as: Parks, unclassified public lands, zoos, museum grounds, historic properties, waterfronts, viewing points, pedestrian malls, boulevards, and open fields. More importantly, however, it might include land used by the public but not a part of the public domain which might be obtained or made available to public use. These areas might include: Vacant lots, alleys, creeks, bayous, natural areas, areas of steep topography, abandoned facilities, and public lands which are currently inaccessible. Within these classifications of public space exists those areas for tennis, basketball, golf, and baseball; however, these are often single purpose and their use must be scheduled. While they are important to a town's recreation program, they often inhibit free and spontaneous use of public space. Public space must include recreation areas; however, it must also include those areas within a town which create image and which offer free choice. These existing and potential public areas constitute the public space environment, which with organization can help create an outstanding public standard of town life.

A plan for these public open spaces includes most of the areas which have been analyzed in PHASE TWO as being important to town character and public enjoyment. What a plan such as this does, in essence, is to create a web of public area or space within which uniqueness preservation and public enjoyment can exist. Private development is thus complemented by this public space structure; and, in turn, will complement town image as projects are undertaken within town guidelines for uniqueness preservation. Advantages of a public open space plan include:

☐ The potential for people's spontaneous enjoyment of a public environment without being programmed or constrained by social or economic factors.

☐ The opportunity for people to live in an environment of positive visual images.

☐ The opportunity to release daily bonds of job or social commitment by relaxing and enjoying moments of freedom and personal quiet.

☐ The opportunity to have social interaction and establish relationships with fellow citizens.

☐ The opportunity to experience nature, such as seasonal change, and to explore oneself through walks along the stream, observing wildlife, or selecting a place to sit.

☐ The opportunity to re-cycle vacant lots, abandoned fields, underused facilities, and old buildings for public use and enjoyment.

☐ And, perhaps, most importantly: **Provides quality leisure time settings outside of the home environment for the full range of town citizens.**[38]

CREATING THE PUBLIC SPACE PLAN

To achieve the previously listed opportunities, should it be determined to follow this OPTION, the town can draw upon existing information from PHASE TWO to create the *Public Space Plan.* This plan should facilitate the inclusion of town uniqueness preservation areas into a townwide effort to achieve a high standard of public living which stresses the quality of public space, space which is open to the freely chosen activity of citizens no matter what their social and economic status.[39]

2.59

2.60

2.59 *The spontaneous and unprogrammed opportunity to use public space is a very important ingredient in unique town settings. Public space preservation should be part of any town's livability and uniqueness preservation activity.*

2.60 *The opportunity for peaceful enjoyment of public space is an important aspect of town character.*

2.61

2.62

2.61 This key open space provides a unique opportunity to experience nature in a spontaneous and relaxed setting.

2.62 The creation of special places within town environments can provide a setting for various activities and events.

The following suggestions do not constitute a detailed planning process; however, it will assist any town which chooses this direction in creating a workable and creative *Public Space Plan*:

1. Create, **with the fullest public participation**, a statement of townwide goals for public space and townwide beautification. Form a Citizens Public Space Committee or add this function to the Town Uniqueness Preservation Committee and conduct workshops on this topic of public space and townwide beautification.

2. Determine the real needs of the people for urban beauty and public space and the reality of how these people use the public environment or how they would like to use it.

3. Determine the existing open space network, including strategically located vacant land. As part of this process conduct a survey of urban beauty in the public environment. Keep in mind that much of this inventory has been done in PHASE TWO and exists as part of the data file system which can be recalled with very little effort.

4. Using this data base and the information concerning citizen needs and desires for public open space, design a townwide Public Space Plan. This plan should include:

   ☐ Public areas indicated on the Town Uniqueness Plan as important to town image

   ☐ A coordinated system of recreation and open space activities

   ☐ Access to views and vistas important to town image

   ☐ Tree plantings which reinforce town image, provide shade, and perhaps even provide seasonal color and/or harvest for public consumption

   ☐ Key linkage opportunities throughout the system which help tie the system into the continuous web.

5. Present the plan to the public and make any changes which are required. Public acceptance is very critical as the Plan must meet their needs and have their support during implementation.

6. No plan such as this can be implemented all at once; therefore, the next step is to establish phases which can be accomplished during each year and which can be realized as part of the town's capital improvements budget. The speed at which this can be accomplished will be affected by the availability of funding, availability of alternate implementation tools, and priorities and needs of the local citizens.

7. Develop a process to monitor the results of the Plan making sure the Plan is kept fresh and meets the original goals as it undergoes implementation.

This *Public Space Plan* will provide a useful structure within which the Town Uniqueness Preservation Committee can propose projects and public land acquisition which will enhance the objectives of the *Town Uniqueness Preservation Plan*.

III. OPTION THREE – SPECIAL DESIGN STUDIES

In PHASE TWO the process analyzed various parts of the town in more detail. These parts were those areas the Team determined to have both a value for town uniqueness preservation and a potential for enhancement, revitalization and designed change. These parts include such areas as: The town square; waterfront areas; clusters of underused historic buildings; existing parts which have ceased to serve their original function; special streets; and unused public land.

Before undertaking these projects a list of potential areas should be created which establishes priorities and determines which areas would better help town image and economic well being. An example might be a waterfront area which would be expensive to upgrade, albeit an important project; but might have less positive impact upon town image than a revitalized town square. This list must remain flexible; however, as economic conditions will often decide which project will be developed. Priorities, therefore, will also need review. The major task at this point is to ensure that these projects are done in harmony with the *Town Uniqueness Preservation Plan*, and that their finished image is positive to overall town image and function. Private developers will play an active role in this process and the Manager should seek them out and introduce them to the various project possibilities. Care, however, must be exercised in the development of these areas. When finished, they should not alter important town functions and should not disrupt the lives of the people who must live in association with them. It is very important for the values and feelings of the town's citizens to be incorporated into the design of these areas.

The approach to each project will vary with circumstances and the degree of difficulty presented by its unique aspects. Once these projects have been identified, be they primarily private development or public, professionals should be engaged to undertake the project. The town's function is to provide the data produced in PHASE TWO, and to provide review during the design and implementation of these projects. The Manager and the Town Uniqueness Preservation Committee should also be familiar with various implementation techniques and tools (See OPTION FOUR) so that they may provide assistance not only at a project's inception, but also during its evolution.

One exception to the use of professionals to undertake the projects is the use of local service clubs and other citizen organizations to undertake such projects as tree planting, clean-up, and minor repairs and paintings. This type of effort has been very successful in many towns and has been the most successful when the effort is organized, part of a larger plan, and is finished within a predetermined time frame.

The importance of the projects outlined in Option Three cannot be overstated. Towns are revitalized in parts, not all at once, and the quality of these projects will make a major impact upon town quality and renewed vitality. The key factor is that the projects fit into a comprehensive whole and remain true to the *spirit of place*. The bibliography of this book lists many case examples of projects which have met the recommended criteria. This list should be reviewed by all participants prior to undertaking specific efforts.

IV. OPTION FOUR –
TOOLS FOR IMPLEMENTATION

Implementation was woven throughout the *Town Uniqueness Preservation Plan's* planning process, and the key implementation activities have been suggested at the end of both PHASE ONE and PHASE TWO. The major aspect of the suggested implementation being the legislative and administrative aspects of the Town Uniqueness Preservation Committee. Therefore, the *Town Uniqueness Preservation Plan* is implemented when it is finished and the Committee and Manager are functioning.

This Option will look at the various tools and techniques which are available to help implement projects after development of the *Town Uniqueness Preservation Plan*. These projects will be those proposed by others or the ones initiated by the Committee. If a planning department is created, and the town follows the course of developing a comprehensive plan; that agency will be or become knowledgeable concerning implementation techniques.

If a planning department is not feasible, the Town Uniqueness Preservation Committee or the Manager can assume the additional task of obtaining this knowledge. In this case the Committee would become an agent for change by encouraging development and by providing knowledge of various techniques which will be useful in accomplishing selected programs and projects. By following this option the Committee goes beyond its original function of reviewing proposed change and determining if that change is compatible with the objectives of the *Town Uniqueness Preservation Plan*.

The tools and techniques which would assist in implementing ideas created in Option Two and Option Three are available at the local level; however, they will vary from state to state, so each town should determine what is available.

The Federal Government also has a myriad of programs available to small towns. Unfortunately these programs frequently change; are not funded with any consistency; are limited to specific tasks; and are difficult for small towns to obtain due to lack of experience and personnel.

The key for successful implementation of various individual projects is to first develop a basic stance concerning implementation and then a basic knowledge of programs, tools, and techniques available to small towns from all sources. Developing the proper stance, or focus, is the key first step. Each Committee or town should know **what it wants to implement** and **what it wants to do**. Gathering together a large variety of implementation tools, or by not carefully matching the tools to the desired implementation results, can often lead to wasted effort. For this reason a framework such as the *Town Uniqueness Preservation Plan* is essential for determining what needs implementation and how the overall objective of town uniqueness preservation can best be served.

Once you know what aspect of the plan is to be implemented, go to a good "tool and technique shop" such as a Council of Governments, State Planning Office, or Federal agency and tell them what needs implementation and what tools you think might help. They will help you to become familiar with the programs best suited to the particular task. Keep in mind: never let existing tools tell you what you can do; and never let the lack of a tool keep you from creating a new one through the political process. Tools, including implementation tools, are artifacts of society's needs, and as needs change new tools are often required. Thus, one option within this task may be to design a new implementation tool, while remembering that existing tools were once new tools. The major point is: a town must first determine, based upon a general knowledge of possibilities, what is to be done and then determine how to do it.

As an overview several major categories of tools are presented in the following list:

SELECTED LISTING OF
FEDERAL AND NATIONAL PROGRAMS

☐ **URBAN DEVELOPMENT ACTION GRANTS** –
For towns under 50,000 people.
Source: The Department of Housing & Urban Development (HUD), Regional Office
Note: These grants require a private sector contribution, the more the better.

□ **SMALL CITIES COMMUNITY DEVELOPMENT BLOCK GRANTS** – Designed for small towns and administered by HUD or directly by state governments.
Source: The Department of Housing and Urban Development or the State Planning Office

□ **HISTORIC PRESERVATION GRANTS-IN-AID** – For surveying and planning activities (not for construction)
Source: The National Park Service of the Department of Interior
Note: Funding is limited to 70 percent of project costs

□ **COMPREHENSIVE PLANNING ASSISTANCE PROGRAM** – Offers planning assistance
Source: Section 701 Planning Grants, a part of Community Development Block Grant Program

□ **COMMUNITY RESOURCE DEVELOPMENT PROGRAM** – Offers various types of assistance to small towns.
Source: State Cooperative Extension Service, Community Resource Development Leader or your local County Extension Agent

□ **URBAN PARKS & RECREATION RECOVERY PROGRAM** – Provides grants to rebuild, develop, and expand existing parks and recreation facilities.
Source: National Park Service, Department of Interior

□ **AREA DEVELOPMENT ASSISTANCE PLANNING GRANTS PROGRAM** – Provides planning assistance for towns of up to 10,000 people with funds up to $50,000.00.
Source: Farmers Home Administration
Note: Offers 75 percent of planning fees.

□ **NATIONAL MAIN STREET PROGRAM** – Provides leadership for small town revitalization.
Source: National Trust for Historic Preservation, Washington, D.C.

SELECTED LISTING OF TOOLS AND TECHNIQUES

□ **FACADE AND SCENIC EASEMENTS** – Purchases made by the community to protect selected image and character.

□ **RESTRICTIVE COVENANTS** – Preservation objectives become a part of the deed to a piece of property.

□ **REVOLVING FUNDS** – A pool of money which provides low interest funding for revitalization and preservation efforts.

□ **PRIVATE FOUNDATIONS** – A source of funding for various activities. Each foundation will have different parameters, however it is best to approach any of these groups with a well conceived program.

□ **SPECIAL DISTRICT OR DOWNTOWN DEVELOPMENT DISTRICT** – This would delineate a particular area which could then undertake a wide variety of planning and revitalization activities as a unified body.[40] [41] [42]

A FINAL NOTE ON OPTIONS – The options presented here are just that, options. Once a town has taken on the *Town Uniqueness Preservation Plan's* process and taken it to a successful completion, it can decide if additional studies are required. The process was designed to produce a plan to protect town character, and to establish a Committee and Manager to enforce that plan's goals through the evaluation of proposed town change. While this is a busy and time consuming role, it is passive in that it only responds to proposed change. In selecting the **options** the Committee and the town assume the more action oriented role of creating a town character and for stimulating new projects in keeping with that character. Each town should be aware that in following the option path, they are going beyond the original goals of this book.

case studies

OVERVIEW

The major case study presented here, **What's So Special About Navasota?**, was conducted simultaneously with the drafting of major portions of this book. Each task, both concept and testing, fed upon the other until the Navasota study was completed. The contents of the final book were then modified by experience gained from Navasota, previous studies, extensive reviews of published town studies, and the observation of many American and European towns facing the problems resulting from growth and change. The ideas expressed in this book have evolved during a period of time and have been sharpened by extensive travel, observation, conversations with town planners in Europe and North America, and a series of town studies conducted and/or supervised by this book's author.

The following brief descriptions of some of these projects will serve to indicate the evolution of the basic ideas expressed in this book, the ideas which were eventually tested in Navasota. In all cases the lessons which were learned from these studies resulted in the revision and refinement of the material which was presented in the previous chapters.

One of the earliest case studies was conducted in Holyoke, Massachusetts. The primary goal of that effort was to understand the character of the town, communicate that character to townspeople, and create a plan to protect special character while undertaking extensive townwide revitalization of poor character. The major focus was upon the Connecticut River, its relationship to the town, its potential as an organizing element, and its potential

role as the primary structure of a townwide open space system. The product which resulted was a townwide open space and selected area revitalization plan. The original structure for this book was a direct outgrowth of the Holyoke prototype.

Following a year in Europe, as a Harvard University Wiedenmen Fellow, studying the impacts of growth and change upon historic small towns, the author had the first opportunity to test the concepts developed in Holyoke. This was done within the scope of the State of Hawaii Comprehensive Open Space Plan which was undertaken for the Overview Corporation. The Hawaii Plan was designed to protect the quality of life in the State by directing growth to protect open space and scenic image.

This pioneer, protypical effort featured many techniques and concepts which were brought together for the first time in a wholistic approach to growth guidance and open space preservation. Four aspects which had a direct bearing on the development of the process presented in Chapter Two were:

1. The use of the basic units, natural, cultural, and visual, as headings for the description and analysis of the State's unique character and open space opportunities. The important aspect was the isolation of visual values and the incorporation of them into the decision making process.

2. The use of a "data file" system to analyze only those aspects of each island which were pertinent, for open space and character protection. This system of over 200 individual

data maps was unique in that it allowed the use of components of a particular data type to be utilized without the unnecessary manipulation of entire data sets.

3. The linkage of plans and programs with special legislation which was designed to facilitate short, medium, and long range implementation tied to government policy.

4. The development of a process for preserving the character of small towns within a larger context. The following excerpt is drawn from the final 1972 report:

> One quality growth concern is the expansion of small towns into their surrounding region. Rapid change, due to sudden zoning changes, proposed major development, etc. can place undue strain upon a town and its region of growth and, so seriously affect its ability to absorb this growth and still retain its character, scale and other attributes which were the root of its original attractiveness. The following is a **recommendation** for dealing with this critical problem and should be applied to such types and scales of towns as Lahaina and Hana, Maui; Wailua and Haleiwa, Oahu; Waimea (Kamuela) and Kailua, Hawaii; and Hanalei, Kauai.
>
> The object is to analyze these towns **before** development pressure is forcing change without proper quality growth guidelines, and the following steps should serve as a guide for that analysis:
>
> 1. Conduct a brief, historical and economic overview of the town to understand its past.
>
> 2. A five-part investigative format should be used to understand the physical ramifications of the town vis-a-vis growth.
>
>   a. Given form: a detailed study of the **town's site and its region – the detailed natural composite.** Understanding should be gained concerning the site's role in shaping the town, historical reasons for the site's selection, and major site features and climate – in short, the total expression of the natural site – the given form.
>
>   b. Made form: a complete understanding of the town's organizational framework should be gained, its districts, paths, nodes (points of gathering), landmarks, and, where possible, the reasoning behind its chosen shape – its plan.
>
>   c. Visual form: analysis of the given form (site and region) plus the made form (plan of the town) should result in an understanding of their interaction – the visual form. This form produces the town's character, its unique expression,

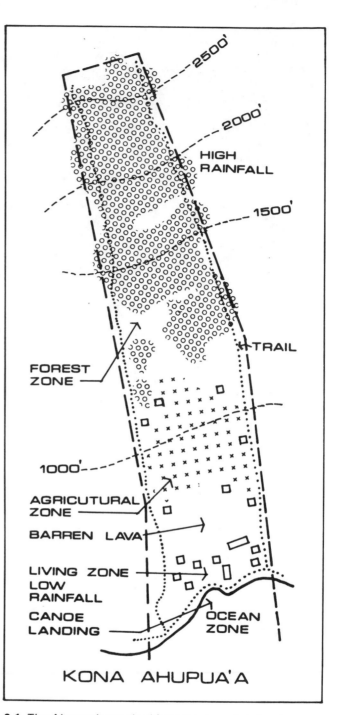

3.1 The Ahupua's reached from the mountain top to the sea. This ancient land division concept established much of Hawaii's original character.

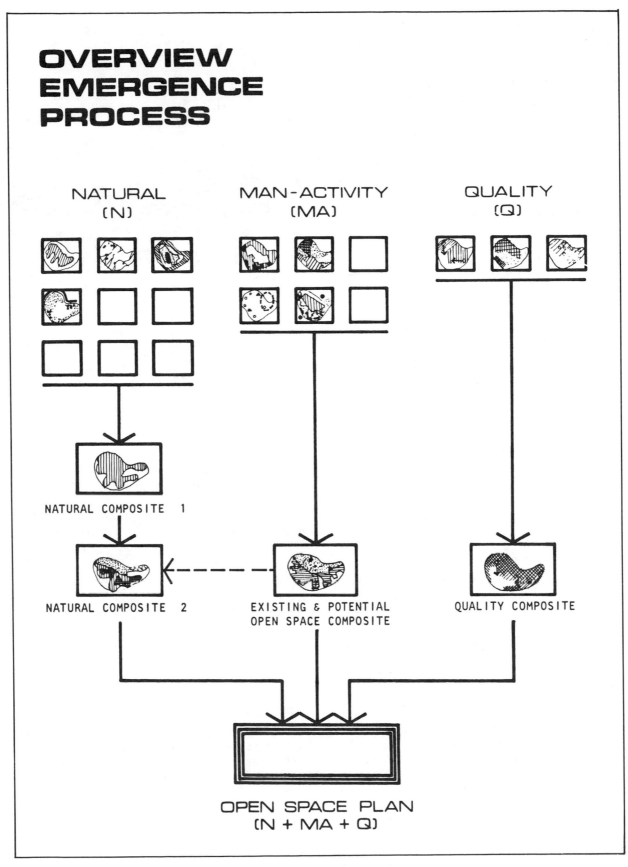

OVERVIEW EMERGENCE PROCESS

NATURAL (N)

MAN-ACTIVITY (MA)

QUALITY (Q)

NATURAL COMPOSITE 1

NATURAL COMPOSITE 2

EXISTING & POTENTIAL OPEN SPACE COMPOSITE

QUALITY COMPOSITE

OPEN SPACE PLAN (N + MA + Q)

3.2 *This diagram indicates the process used to create the Hawaii Open Space Plan.*

its **Genius Loci***. This must be understood to determine how growth should occur without destroying the town's character.*

   d. Parts: after the total form of a town is understood vis-a-vis its region of potential growth, a detailed analysis of the town's parts should be undertaken to determine the role they should play in future growth. Analysis should be done of the major streets, open spaces, landmarks, entrances, etc., to understand their individual function and visual expression and the role they play in the total visual image of the town. Essentially this is a study, using the techniques of morphological analysis (an analytical technique developed by E. F. Sekler), of the open spaces, the mass that defines them, and the links that tie them together.

   e. Activities: an understanding of the activities that happen within the form or have happened historically, and the attitudes of the actors (citizens) concerning the rightness of the existing form or the desire for future variations should be gained. These investigations would go beyond recorded land use to the myriad of interconnected happenings that give life to the town.

  3. Based upon this analysis the State and County should articulate those growth and physical design guidelines for the town to insure its proper future relationship to the Open Space Plan, and statewide quality growth policy.

  4. Land use controls and urban design concepts should be determined to implement these growth guidelines.

   This book's concepts were further tested by studies conducted in Harrisville, New Hampshire; Vinton, Virginia; Goochland, Virginia; Charlottesville, Virginia; San Marcos, Texas; Medina, Texas; Dibol, Texas; and Bolivar Peninsula, Texas. The Navasota case study, which follows, was the summation and testing of those ideas developed during the various studies and projects.

3.3

3.4

3.3 *The well-defined town surrounded by agricultural fields is a positive aspect of Hawaii's rural image. The sugar mill stack issues forth non-polluting water vapor.*

3.4 *This town has been transformed by suburban sprawl; its character has been lost; and the silent mill indicates that the agricultural fields have been developed for subdivisions.*

3.5

3.5 New development which acknowledges cultural diversity has been a positive influence upon town environments.

3.6 Sunset and historic images provide much of Lahaina Maui's spirit of place.

3.6

WHAT'S SO SPECIAL ABOUT NAVASOTA?

A Townscape Preservation and Enhancement Program for Navasota, Texas

3.7 *Navasota's unique past is indicated by its monuments and distinctive architecture.*

INTRODUCTION – THE BACKGROUND AND THE PROCESS

The project described in this case study is the result of a grant from the National Endowment for the Arts, American Architectural Heritage Program, to the town of Navasota, Texas. Work was undertaken in three phases, beginning in June of 1977 and culminating June, 1978. PHASE ONE dealt with initial organization, citizen participation sessions, and early town character assessment. PHASE TWO developed an extensive analytical base and produced townwide conclusions and recommendations. PHASE THREE revised all previous work, finalized the townwide recommendations, and developed detailed design guidelines and implementation suggestions.

The goal of the project was to enhance and preserve not only historic or unique town fabric, but also to maintain the spirit of that fabric as the town undergoes inevitable and desirable growth and change. Navasota was a perfect choice for this study because it is:

- Within one hour commute of Houston, Texas, and is undergoing growth as a permanent and second home location for Houston people desiring small town or country life.

- Near a major tourist destination area being planned 9 miles to the west at Washington on the Brazos State Park (the site of the signing of the Texas Declaration of Independence). The impact upon Navasota will be significant and the potential for disruptive change is very high.

- Located in a very historic area of Texas.

- A unique townscape in very good order with fine old homes and commercial structures.

- A vital downtown which serves as the commercial center for the surrounding region.

- Undertaking a new planning and zoning study which would be positively influenced by the nature of the study suggested by this proposal.

- Located in a unique natural setting with the surrounding landscape some of the finest in Central Texas.

- A study area at the right moment of time to decide its future, how it will protect its uniqueness and how much needed economic growth might occur without destroying its existing character.

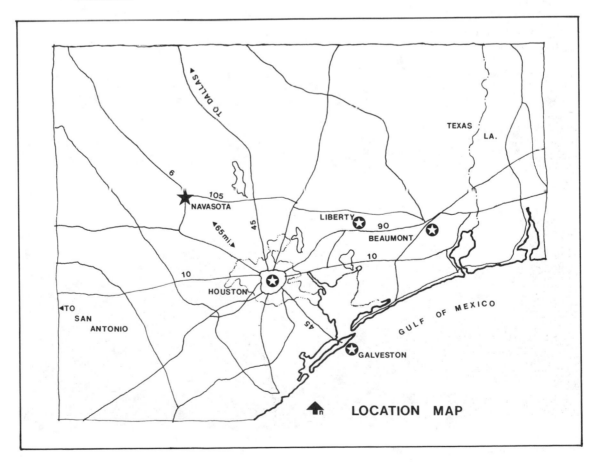

LOCATION MAP

3.8 Aerial view of Navasota

3.9 Visual landmark

3.10 Church steeples dominate the visual image of the Navasota skyline.

Process

This project was conducted by a design process which was conceived to meet the two major goals of this effort: *Unique town character protection and citizen participation*. The following process diagram indicates the basic steps in this planning and design effort and the chapters of this report indicate the activities and conclusions of each step.

Citizen participation during the project covered the full range of types including *public meetings, workshops, presentations, questionnaires* and many *individual conversations*. The major points of citizen interaction are indicated on the process diagram, however, in fact the interaction was continuous and happened whenever it wanted to or needed to.

Local newspapers, the Bryan Eagle and the Navasota Examiner, provided invaluable assistance to the project goal of public participation. The several news stories they published served to inform citizens during this phase and increase their awareness of the project. Another key aspect of this phase was the printing of a short questionnaire in the Navasota Examiner which allowed all citizens to participate in the communication process.

DIAGRAM A: PROCESS

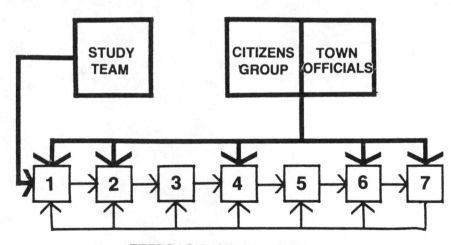

FEEDBACK AND REVISION

1 **Goals and Values**
2 **Search for Uniqueness**
3 **Inventory and Analysis**
4 **Navasota Uniqueness Preservation Plan**
5 **Navasota Public Space Plan**
6 **Implementation**
7 **Monitor and Update Process**

3.11 *Church Street vista – a key character ingredient*

STEP ONE — GOALS AND VALUES

INTRODUCTION

Early in the project, a workshop was held with the Navasota Citizen Advisory Committee. During this session, the staff presented a series of ideas concerning the project for comment and review by the committee members. At this session a questionnaire was also distributed to further define citizen value understanding. The goal of these early efforts was to inform the citizens about the project and allow the study team to understand citizen values and opinions concerning town uniqueness and character. As a result of these sessions the following basic assumptions and project goals were agreed upon jointly by the citizens committee, city officials and the study team.

Basic Assumptions

1. The people of Navasota desire to be involved in the project.
2. Navasota will grow in population and area.
3. The downtown will remain the major economic-commercial center of town.
4. Historic buildings and town fabric will be protected.
5. A major open space will be developed along Cedar Creek.
6. Trees are good and should be maintained or planted.
7. Navasota will become a tourist destination area as a result of its proximity to Washington-on-the-Brazos State Park.
8. Design solutions resulting from this project will suit the needs of Navasota because they will have had citizen input and support from the beginning.

Project Goals

1. Encourage local citizens to participate in the project and keep them informed through public meetings and newspaper reports.
2. Identify the desires and goals of the citizens with regard to growth and change in Navasota.
3. Identify and maintain those qualities and characteristics of Navasota that its citizens want to preserve.
4. Identify the types of change and locations of potential change that affect Navasota.
5. Provide a frame of reference for townwide planning and zoning which would insure that the qualitative aspects of appearance and town image would be preserved.
6. Preserve and enhance the appearance of downtown Navasota.
7. Provide a pleasant and safe experience for both pedestrians and motorists in the downtown area.
8. Develop a comprehensive plan which can be implemented as a series of short-term projects.
9. Achieve implementation.
10. Play upon the historic setting.
11. Do work of high quality, using the most advanced tools and techniques.

REGIONAL SETTING

Concurrent with the citizens meetings and questionnaire analysis the team developed an understanding of Navasota's regional setting to better understand the town context. Assessment indicated that Navasota is located on the western edge of Grimes County near the confluence of the Navasota and Brazos Rivers. Most of the county lies in the Post Oak Savannah of the East Texas Timberlands with a small area of Blackland Prairie in the central portion. Natural resources in the county include oil, gas, stone and lignite. Extraction of lignite and construction of a power generating plant in central Grimes County will begin in the near future. Agriculture is the dominant land use, accounting for over 70 percent of the total land area. Because of the dairy farming, which puts Grimes County near the top in the number of dairy farms in the state, and the Weaver Apiaries, which ships bees and honey all over the U.S. and to foreign countries, Grimes County is now known as "the land of milk and honey." The county is rich in historic sites, many of which are listed on the National Register of Historic Places or the State Historic Preservation List. Navasota is the gateway to Washington-on-the-Brazos State Park, a 71-acre park in Washington County where the Texas Declaration of Independence was signed before the war with Mexico and where the Constitution of the Republic of Texas was adopted in 1836. It was also the capital of the Republic of Texas on two occasions. The Bureau of Census estimated the population of Grimes County to be 12,500 in 1974. The ethnic make-up of the population is 10% Mexican-American, 35% Black and 55% Anglo. About 5,000 people live in Navasota. An excellent highway system links the county with the major market centers in Texas. Navasota has access to rail and motor freight service, commercial bus lines and private aircraft facilities. The Amtrak passenger rail lines can be boarded in Brenham, a short distance to the west in Washington County.

NAVASOTA: BASIC CHARACTER

The town itself also underwent initial assessment of its character ingredients. Asking the question "What's special about Navasota?" the study team conducted a quick first visual impression. Navasota was examined by looking at the town from the countryside and looking at the countryside from inside the town; noting the main entrance points and key points of arrival within the town; an inventory of major streets, businesses and public spaces within the town; a more detailed look at downtown and finally a close look at the town's materials, the parts that bind it together like sidewalks, plantings and lighting.

This early assessment resulted in the following basic statement of Navasota's special character. Since its founding, the character of Navasota has been shaped primarily by three forces: crossroads, railroad and rich farmland. Navasota's bustling downtown commercial center is the focus of its crossroads — town image, which is as strong in the present days of Highway 6 as in the days of the La Bahia Road. Its turn-of-the-century, railroad town image is reinforced by the architectural style of the downtown commercial structures, many of which were built between 1870 and 1930; and by the physical presence of passing trains. The fine old homes with mature trees shading well-kept yards and the churches constructed of local stone with an unusual mortar finish are essential elements in Navasota's image; as is Cedar Creek, which bisects the town. The country lifestyle of "the land of milk and honey" permeates the town, with open land and backyard farms penetrating from all directions.

While based upon a certain combination of three key ingredients — crossroads, railroad and farmland — Navasota's basic character is that of a small, typically Texan, town whose central image, worn smooth by the passage of time, just needs a good polish, especially around the edges where growth and change tug at its cohesiveness. In an attempt to locate this character a map was created, see map "Character One," which shows where certain aspects of Navasota's townwide uniqueness are located. Citizen reaction to the information displayed on the map and a summary of the questionnaire results indicated the need for additional efforts toward initial town character identification. This became the next task of the study team.

3.12 Existing image – typical of main street Navasota

3.13 The land of milk and honey

3.14 Cedar Creek – a key open space element

3.15 Downtown Navasota

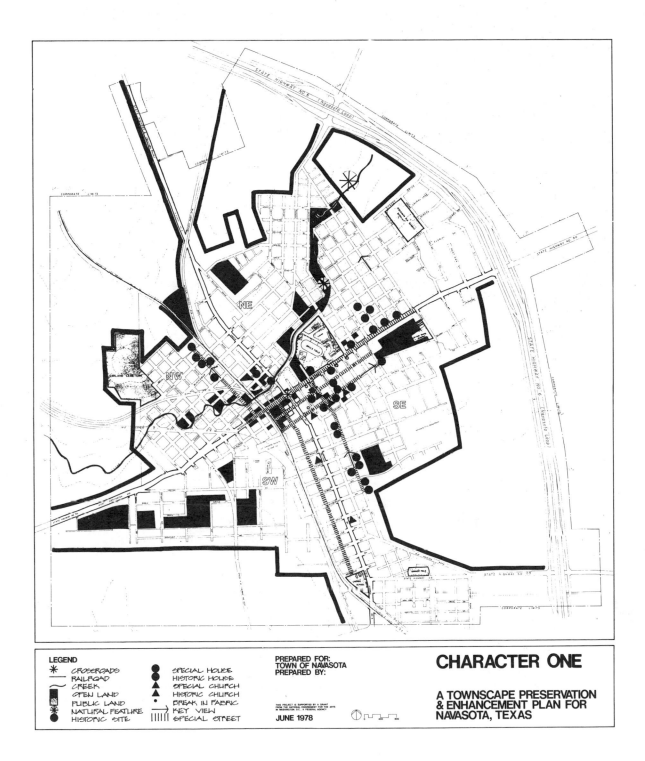

STEP TWO — SEARCH FOR UNIQUENESS

Analysis of workshop and questionnaire information as presented in Step One, resulted in the creation of a second and third character map of Navasota. These maps served as the basis for the more detailed analysis needed to locate the ingredients of uniqueness areas. While these maps are very important and they show the basic character of Navasota, they do not place relative values upon the different aspects of these character producing ingredients. For example, the maps indicate that certain streets are special and that the town creek is also special, what it *does not* do however is say which areas are more special than others.

The next phase of this project created more detailed analysis which allowed the team to set values and say which areas were the most special and therefore which areas needed careful attention. The key aspect of the character map phase is that it identifies the data which requires more analysis and mapping, while also indicating that information which does not need mapping. This information allowed the team to avoid extensive mapping of unwanted data while allowing them to single out only that information which is relevant to town character producing ingredients. The following list suggests those things Navasota people felt were special about Navasota which could be displayed on maps. Maps "Character Two" and the final "Character Three" indicate the items on this list.

Historic House, Church & Site — state or national historic marker is located on building or site.

Point of Interest — citizen questionnaire response to "what places would you show an out-of-town guest?"

Open Land — land showing little or no manipulation by man; as well as vacant, unbuilt land within major builtup areas.

Natural Features — natural element, because of its occurrence in the surrounding town fabric, is unusual and stands apart as an identifiable entity.

Impact of Change — specific point where visual impact of change in use, scale, form, siting, etc., is dominant and disturbing.

Entry Point — point at which most residents feel they enter town.

Key View — particularly good views of significant character producing elements.

Special House and/or Church — cannot be easily replaced or reproduced because of architectural style, type of material or quality of workmanship.

Special Street — mentioned 5 or more times on citizen questionnaire as one of the nicest streets; possesses common visual elements, such as: well maintained yards and homes; old, historic homes; new houses, churches; clean streets; well lighted public areas; paved streets; sidewalks; pedestrian facilities; trees, shade, color; good views.

Good Street — mentioned more than once but fewer than five times; possesses some of the above ingredients.

Street with Potential — mentioned only once; but possesses some of the ingredients of a special street but needs improvement, especially due to location in relation to town layout and function.

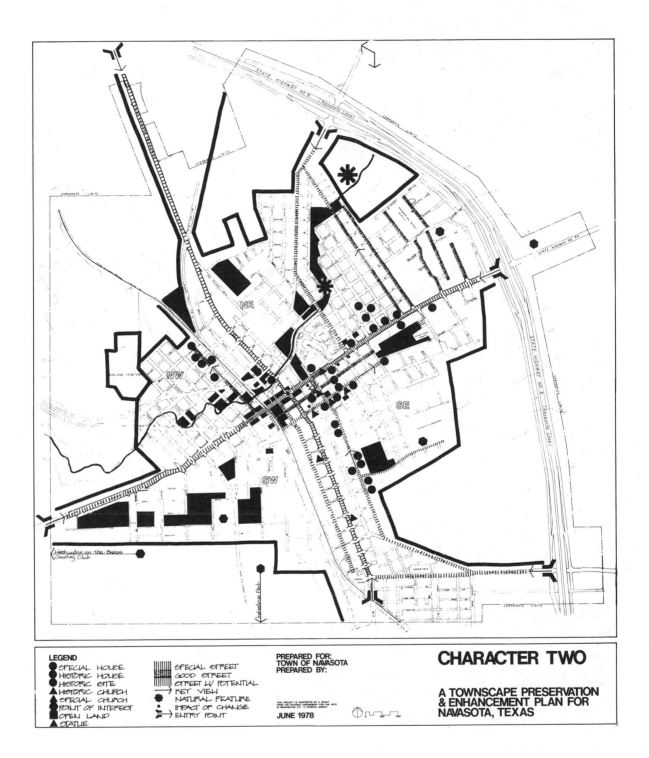

3.16 *Historic commercial store fronts provide character and restoration potential.*

3.17 *Well kept homes are a Navasota feature.*

3.18 *Railroad Avenue – buildings provide the image for this special town district.*

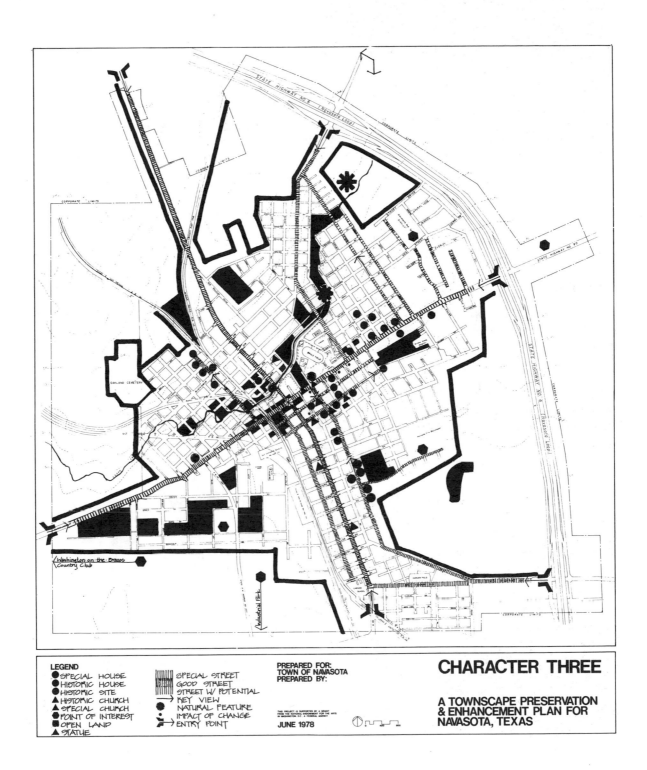

PREPARED FOR:
TOWN OF NAVASOTA
PREPARED BY:

THIS PROJECT IS SUPPORTED BY A GRANT
FROM THE NATIONAL ENDOWMENT FOR THE ARTS
IN WASHINGTON, D.C. A FEDERAL AGENCY.

JUNE 1978

LEGEND
● SPECIAL HOUSE
● HISTORIC HOUSE
● HISTORIC SITE
▲ HISTORIC CHURCH
▲ SPECIAL CHURCH
● POINT OF INTEREST
■ OPEN LAND
▲ STATUE

▥ SPECIAL STREET
▥ GOOD STREET
STREET W/ POTENTIAL
→ KEY VIEW
● NATURAL FEATURE
IMPACT OF CHANGE
→ ENTRY POINT

CHARACTER THREE

A TOWNSCAPE PRESERVATION & ENHANCEMENT PLAN FOR NAVASOTA, TEXAS

STEP THREE — INVENTORY - ANALYSIS

INTRODUCTION

The following section illustrates the detailed analysis and mapping conducted in Navasota concerning the *natural, cultural,* and *visual* realms and the role they play in creating town uniqueness. This material was gathered by on-site visits, conversations, analysis of existing maps and the interpretation of infrared aerial photography. These maps are described in this step and the actual maps are on file with the Navasota Community Development Director. The major reason for this activity was to specifically locate and map the town uniqueness ingredients mentioned in the questionnaire and indicated on the town character maps. Once this material was located and mapped the relationships between various aspects could be determined and values could be assigned to the different uniqueness ingredients. This activity of assigning values will be presented in a forthcoming step which explains how all of the data was brought together to create a town uniqueness preservation and enhancement plan for Navasota.

Natural Systems

The work of nature has affected the town of Navasota and has created some of its special character. The list of natural ingredients involved in the town's composition is quite long, however certain key natural elements were selected as the prime image producers for Navasota. These aspects are described in the following list.

Topography Map No. 1 — This information was mapped to illustrate the general topography in 20' levels of elevation. Its major role was to locate high points and to indicate the slope of the land within the town.

Surface Water Map No. 2 — This map was created to locate surface water and adjacent floodplains as well as visible stock ponds. Surface water was judged as very important to a town's image.

Natural Areas Map No. 3 — All shaded areas on this map indicate either high levels of vegetation or surface water that have not been noticeably altered by man. These areas are well suited for wildlife habitat and have a high potential for public use.

Unique Natural Features Map No. 4 — This map indicates trees that are particularly large, that contribute shade and scale to a street or building, or give special character to a space because of its siting. Navasota's unique features include a large pecan grove and a rock outcropping on Cedar Creek.

Vegetation Densities Map No. 5 — Areas of high density are most natural in appearance and contain trees, underbrush and groundcover. Medium density indicates largely neighborhoods that possess trees and grass with other plants, while low density areas have few if any trees and little or no groundcover. Vegetation density plays a major positive role in the creation of town uniqueness.

Cultural Systems

Cultural systems in the context of this report examine man's interaction with the natural site during the evolution of the town and look at people's past and present activities. The goal is to discover those unique aspects of Navasota which are an outgrowth of her citizen's activities and upon which they have assigned positive values.

The following information was evaluated during this phase.

Land Use Map No. 6 — This map identifies the boundaries of various types of land use activities taking place within the town.

Land Ownership Map No. 7 — Lands owned by the public, private and quasi-public (institutional) are shown on this map.

Phases of Growth Map No. 8 — Navasota experienced three major growth phases, those being the original town layout dictated by the H & TC Railroad, the post-1900 growth era, and the series of developments which began after World War II and continued to the present.

Historic Resources Map No. 9 — Historic buildings and monuments contribute towards the cultural uniqueness of Navasota and lend a special character to the area in which they are located.

Transportation Network Map No. 10 — This identifies the hierarchy of traffic throughout the town, including the city right-of-ways.

Existing Infrastructure Map No. 11 — This map locates the different cultural elements essential to the active functioning of the town, including administrative, social and public service facilities.

Town Structure Map No 12 — Navasota has distinctive components, such as landmarks, gathering points (nodes), edges and paths that make up the town structure and give the town its unique image. One of the most important aspects of this map is its indication of the various activities which exist in Navasota. It locates the various cafes, bars, restaurants, barber shops, small stores and other spots where people gather. These places provide much of Navasota's image and serve as important cultural and ethnic expressions of town uniqueness and identity.

Visual Systems

The final aspect of townwide analysis deals with visual quality and town appearance. Town appearance results from the physical interaction of people with the town's site and in most cases its the visual perception of this interaction which establishes a town's image or character in people's minds. This effort sought out the positive and negative visual aspects of Navasota, and organized them for future decision-making relative to town appearance.

Visual Analysis Map No. 13 — This map identifies the individual areas and points of visual interest in the town.

Visual Elements:

Panorama — unlimited view over a wide area.

Vista — view of a visual objective or focal point and beyond, directed by partially enclosing or framing elements.

Closed Vista — view stops at focal point.

Unpleasant View — visual clutter, trash, wires, poor maintenance, broken paved areas, large signs.

Potential View — existing view or vista capable of being developed as a pleasant visual experience.

Glimpse — brief, hasty, partial view of a landmark, focal point or some visual objective.

Views to; Water — views or glimpses of the creek or other bodies of water.

Open Space — views to open or undeveloped land, especially where these view reinforce the concept of "the country-in-the-city."

Landmarks — points or orientation, generally unique (for their surroundings) and memorable.

Focal Point — object upon which a view converges.

Events: *Gathering Place* — a location or space where people converge and interact.

Pedestrian activity — areas with a high frequency of movement, even if the people do not interact.

Gateway — an obvious entrance to a distinct area.

Entry Point — a spot at which the people feel they have "entered" Navasota.

Sidewalks — Sidewalk development indicating demand for pedestrian facilities.

Impact of Change — points where the visual impact of a structure or facility is distracting; points out of context with the surrounding town fabric or image.

Dead End — Streets that force user to turn 180' to leave the area.

Special Streets and Places Map No. 14 — The areas marked "*Special Streets*" on this map, have been identified in the questionnaire as special. Indicating these streets serve two purposes. First, they create a set of examples from which individual design items that create a sense of uniqueness can be derived. Second, if the designer and public agree they can be preserved *as is*, as special places. It is also of interest that the "*Special Streets*" often capsulize the essence of a particular neighborhood or district.

Breaks in Fabric are imaginary boundaries between districts of unified image. When one crosses a break in fabric he should notice a distinct change in the character of the area.

Special areas are districts with a unified image that the people of Navasota have indicated as "special," "different" and often "better" than the rest of the city.

Buildings essential to function are those buildings which serve Navasota in a functional manner. They may not be particularly unique to Navasota nor an important part of its image, they do play an important role in establishing orientation and identity for the community.

Buildings essential to image are those buildings which the citizens have indicated or which the survey shows are characteristic to the image unique to Navasota. These buildings are recognized are being "special," generally due to their architecture or siting.

Good views are those views that play an especially important part in earning a street or district the "special" rating.

3.19 Fine homes terminate views on many of Navasota's special streets.

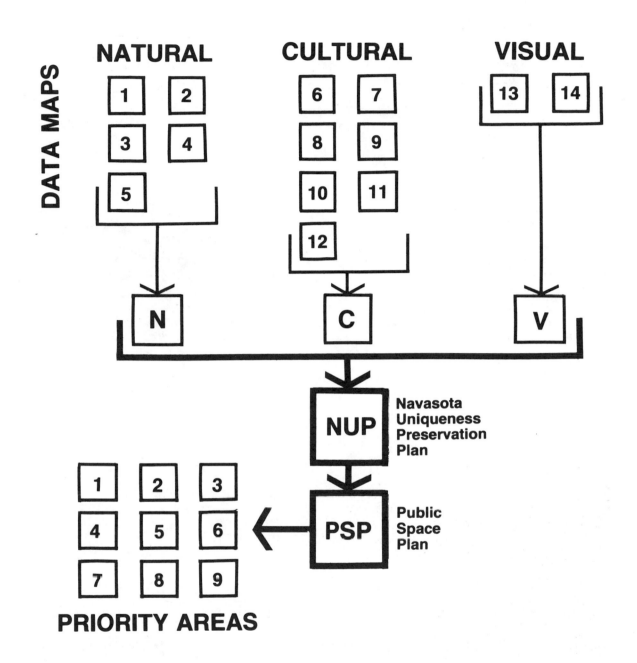

DATA MAPS

NATURAL

| 1 | 2 |
| 3 | 4 |
| 5 |

N

CULTURAL

6	7
8	9
10	11
12

C

VISUAL

| 13 | 14 |

V

NUP — Navasota Uniqueness Preservation Plan

PSP — Public Space Plan

1	2	3
4	5	6
7	8	9

PRIORITY AREAS

DIAGRAM B: MAPPING

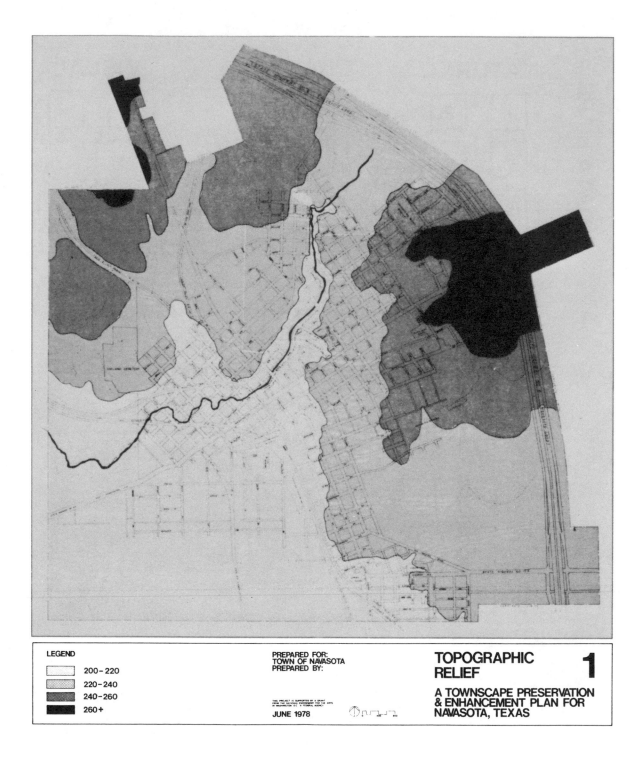

LEGEND

	200 – 220
	220 – 240
	240 – 260
	260+

PREPARED FOR:
TOWN OF NAVASOTA
PREPARED BY:

THIS PROJECT IS SUPPORTED BY A GRANT
FROM THE NATIONAL ENDOWMENT FOR THE ARTS,
IN WASHINGTON D.C. A FEDERAL AGENCY

JUNE 1978

TOPOGRAPHIC
RELIEF   1

A TOWNSCAPE PRESERVATION
& ENHANCEMENT PLAN FOR
NAVASOTA, TEXAS

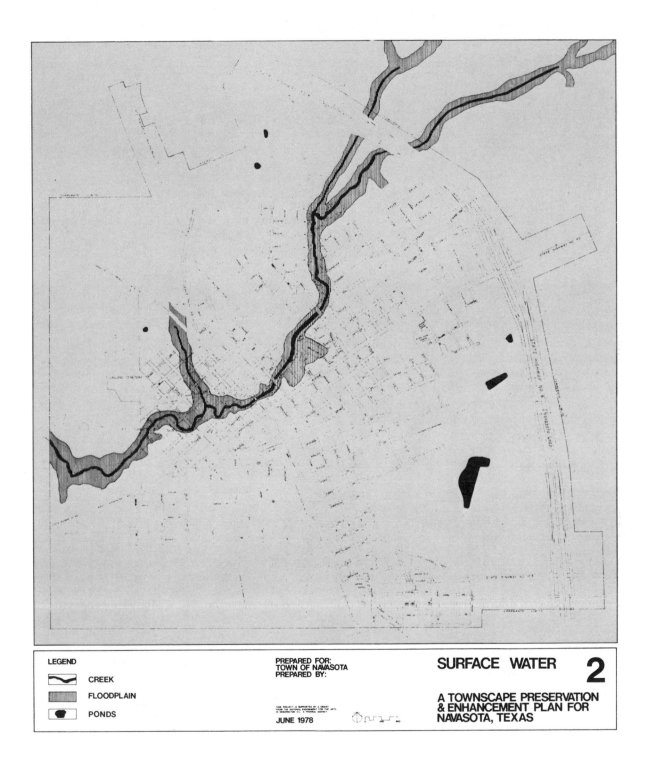

LEGEND

〜 CREEK

▥ FLOODPLAIN

🌑 PONDS

PREPARED FOR:
TOWN OF NAVASOTA
PREPARED BY:

THIS PROJECT IS SUPPORTED BY A GRANT
FROM THE NATIONAL ENDOWMENT FOR THE ARTS
IN WASHINGTON D.C. A FEDERAL AGENCY

JUNE 1978

SURFACE WATER   2

A TOWNSCAPE PRESERVATION
& ENHANCEMENT PLAN FOR
NAVASOTA, TEXAS

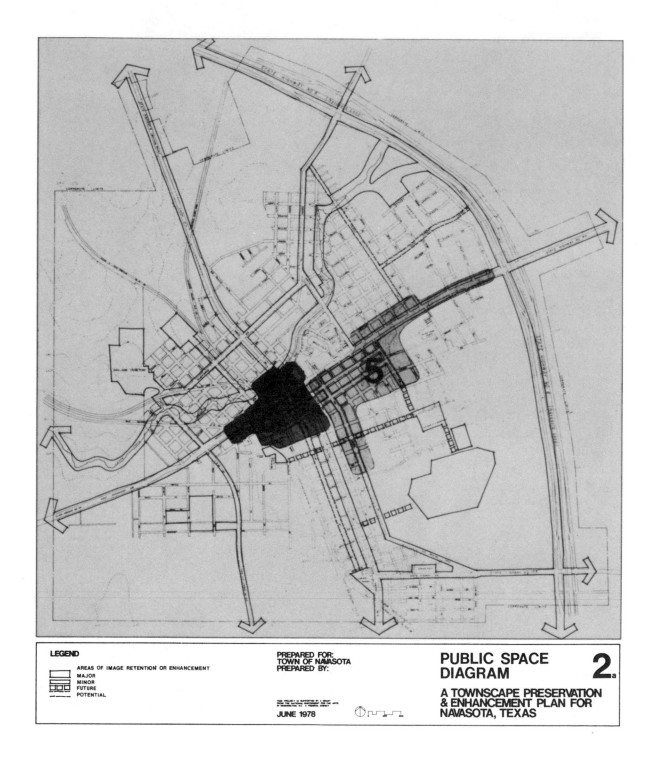

PREPARED FOR:
TOWN OF NAVASOTA
PREPARED BY:

THIS PROJECT IS SUPPORTED BY A GRANT
FROM THE NATIONAL ENDOWMENT FOR THE ARTS
IN WASHINGTON D.C. A FEDERAL AGENCY

JUNE 1978

PUBLIC SPACE
DIAGRAM   2a

A TOWNSCAPE PRESERVATION
& ENHANCEMENT PLAN FOR
NAVASOTA, TEXAS

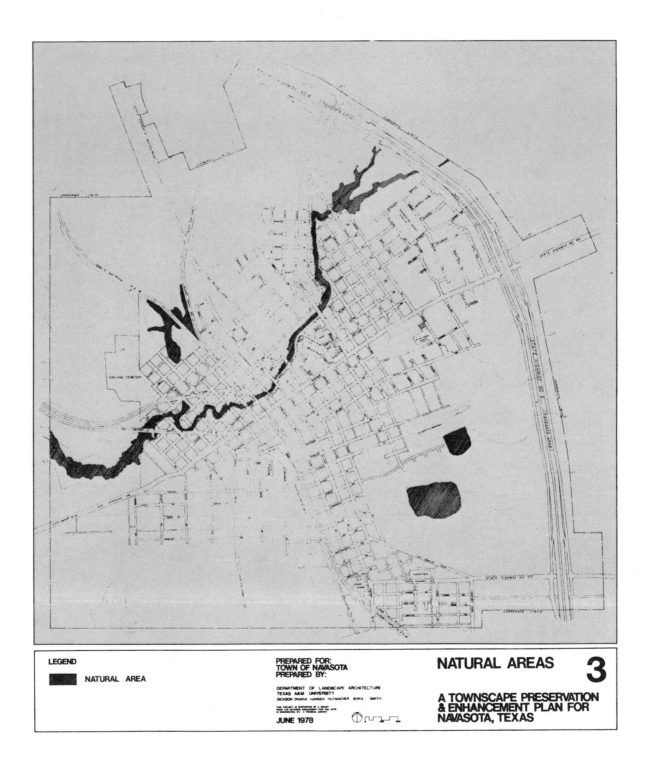

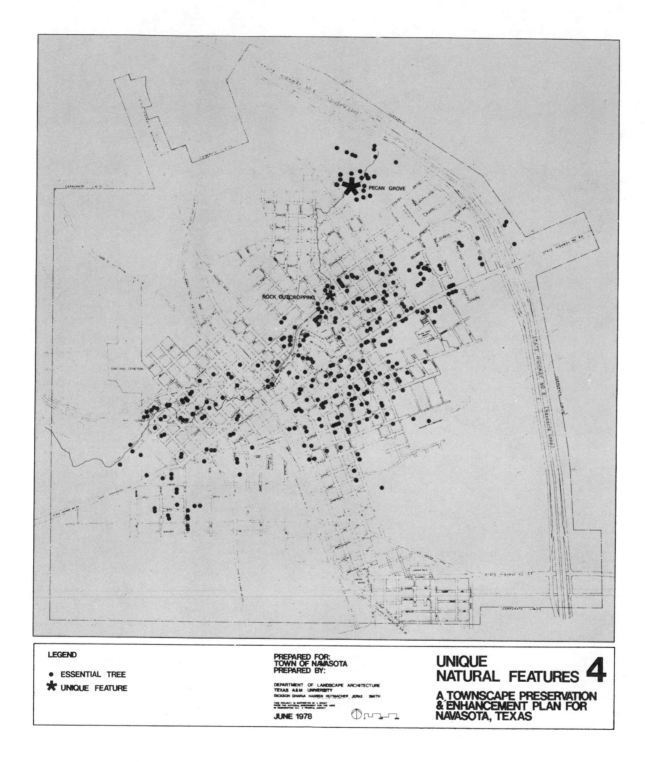

PREPARED FOR:
TOWN OF NAVASOTA
PREPARED BY:

DEPARTMENT OF LANDSCAPE ARCHITECTURE
TEXAS A&M UNIVERSITY
DICKSON DHARIA HARBEN HUTMACHER JERLE SMITH

THIS PROJECT IS SUPPORTED BY A GRANT
FROM THE NATIONAL ENDOWMENT FOR THE ARTS
IN WASHINGTON, D.C. A FEDERAL AGENCY

JUNE 1978

UNIQUE
NATURAL FEATURES 4

A TOWNSCAPE PRESERVATION & ENHANCEMENT PLAN FOR NAVASOTA, TEXAS

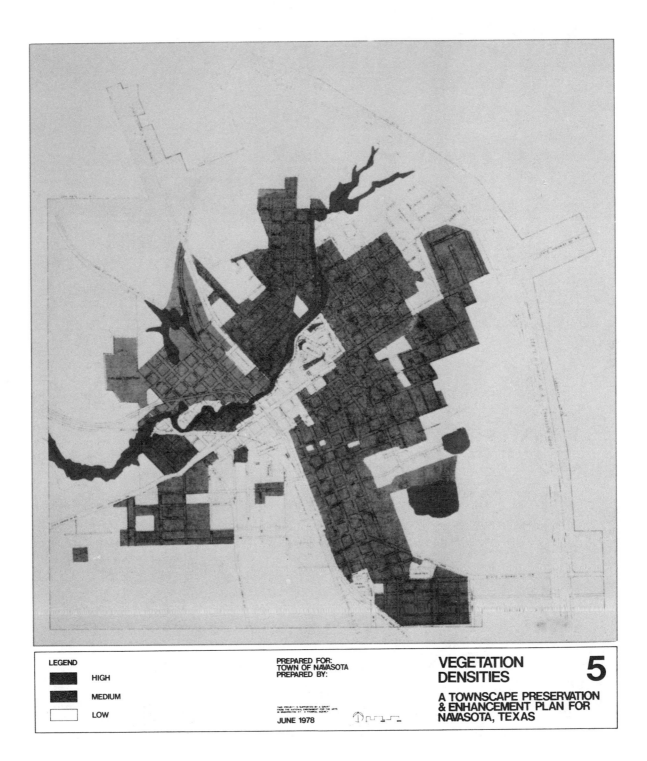

PREPARED FOR:
TOWN OF NAVASOTA
PREPARED BY:

THIS PROJECT IS SUPPORTED BY A GRANT
FROM THE NATIONAL ENDOWMENT FOR THE ARTS
IN WASHINGTON D.C. A FEDERAL AGENCY

JUNE 1978

VEGETATION
DENSITIES   5

A TOWNSCAPE PRESERVATION
& ENHANCEMENT PLAN FOR
NAVASOTA, TEXAS

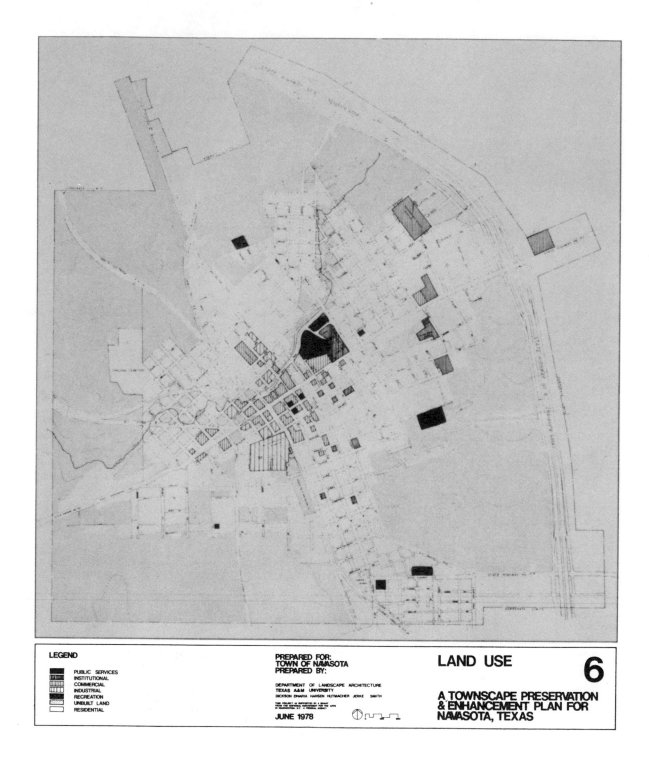

PREPARED FOR:
TOWN OF NAVASOTA
PREPARED BY:

DEPARTMENT OF LANDSCAPE ARCHITECTURE
TEXAS A&M UNIVERSITY
DICKSON DHARIA HANSEN HUTMACHER JERKE SMITH

THIS PROJECT IS SUPPORTED BY A GRANT
FROM THE NATIONAL ENDOWMENT FOR THE ARTS
IN WASHINGTON, D.C. A FEDERAL AGENCY

JUNE 1978

LAND USE   6

A TOWNSCAPE PRESERVATION & ENHANCEMENT PLAN FOR NAVASOTA, TEXAS

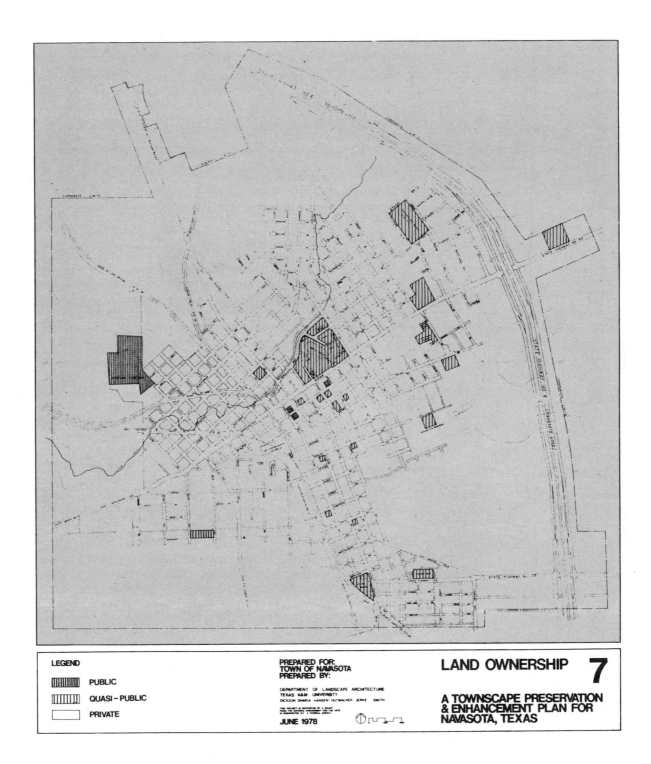

PREPARED FOR:
TOWN OF NAVASOTA
PREPARED BY:

DEPARTMENT OF LANDSCAPE ARCHITECTURE
TEXAS A&M UNIVERSITY
DICKSON DHARIA HANSEN HUTMACHER JERKE SMITH

THIS PROJECT IS SUPPORTED BY A GRANT
FROM THE NATIONAL ENDOWMENT FOR THE ARTS
IN WASHINGTON D.C. A FEDERAL AGENCY

JUNE 1978

LAND OWNERSHIP **7**

A TOWNSCAPE PRESERVATION
& ENHANCEMENT PLAN FOR
NAVASOTA, TEXAS

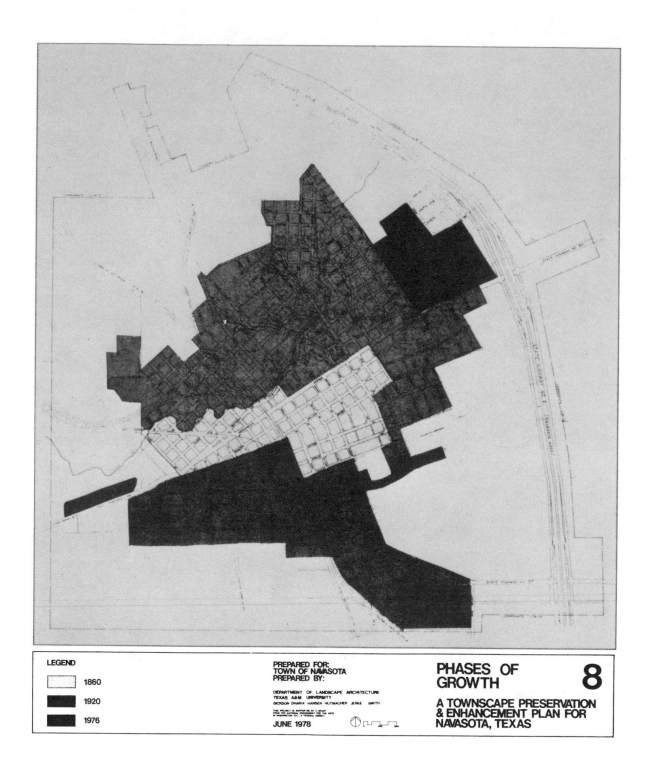

PREPARED FOR:
TOWN OF NAVASOTA
PREPARED BY:

DEPARTMENT OF LANDSCAPE ARCHITECTURE
TEXAS A&M UNIVERSITY
DICKSON DHARIA HANSEN HUTMACHER JERKE SMITH

THIS PROJECT IS SUPPORTED BY A GRANT
FROM THE NATIONAL ENDOWMENT FOR THE ARTS
IN WASHINGTON, D.C. A FEDERAL AGENCY

JUNE 1978

PHASES OF
GROWTH   8

A TOWNSCAPE PRESERVATION
& ENHANCEMENT PLAN FOR
NAVASOTA, TEXAS

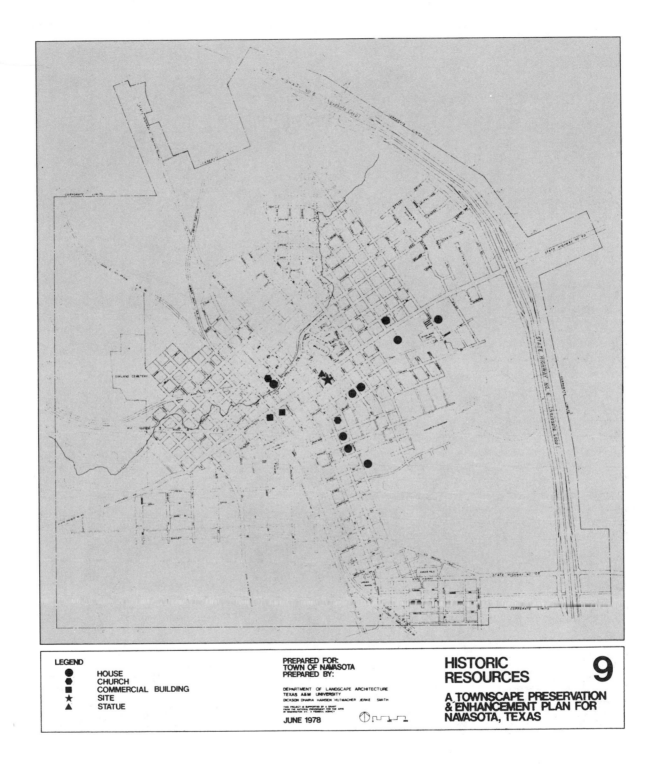

LEGEND

● HOUSE
● CHURCH
■ COMMERCIAL BUILDING
★ SITE
▲ STATUE

PREPARED FOR:
TOWN OF NAVASOTA
PREPARED BY:

DEPARTMENT OF LANDSCAPE ARCHITECTURE
TEXAS A&M UNIVERSITY
DICKSON DHARIA HANSEN HUTMACHER JERKE SMITH

THIS PROJECT IS SUPPORTED BY A GRANT
FROM THE NATIONAL ENDOWMENT FOR THE ARTS
IN WASHINGTON D.C. A FEDERAL AGENCY

JUNE 1978

HISTORIC
RESOURCES 9

A TOWNSCAPE PRESERVATION
& ENHANCEMENT PLAN FOR
NAVASOTA, TEXAS

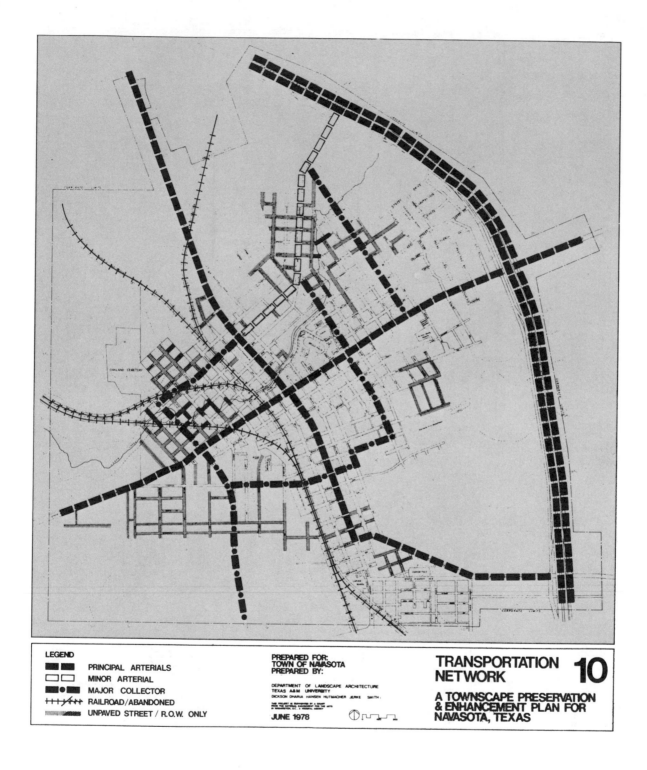

PREPARED FOR:
TOWN OF NAVASOTA
PREPARED BY:

DEPARTMENT OF LANDSCAPE ARCHITECTURE
TEXAS A&M UNIVERSITY
DICKSON DHARIA HANSEN HUTMACHER JEWKE SMITH

THIS PROJECT IS SUPPORTED BY A GRANT
FROM THE NATIONAL ENDOWMENT FOR THE ARTS
IN WASHINGTON, D.C. A FEDERAL AGENCY

JUNE 1978

**TRANSPORTATION
NETWORK** **10**

**A TOWNSCAPE PRESERVATION
& ENHANCEMENT PLAN FOR
NAVASOTA, TEXAS**

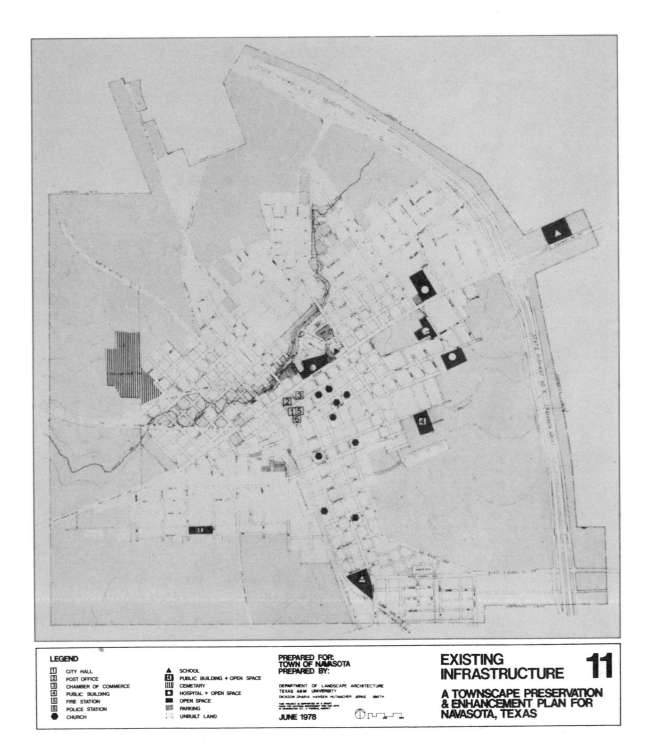

LEGEND

1 CITY HALL
2 POST OFFICE
3 CHAMBER OF COMMERCE
4 PUBLIC BUILDING
5 FIRE STATION
6 POLICE STATION
● CHURCH

▲ SCHOOL
4 PUBLIC BUILDING + OPEN SPACE
||||| CEMETARY
◆ HOSPITAL + OPEN SPACE
■ OPEN SPACE
▨ PARKING
▨ UNBUILT LAND

PREPARED FOR:
TOWN OF NAVASOTA
PREPARED BY:

DEPARTMENT OF LANDSCAPE ARCHITECTURE
TEXAS A&M UNIVERSITY
DICKSON DHARIA HANSEN HUTMACHER JERKE SMITH

THIS PROJECT IS SUPPORTED BY A GRANT
FROM THE NATIONAL ENDOWMENT FOR THE ARTS
IN WASHINGTON, D.C. A FEDERAL AGENCY

JUNE 1978

EXISTING INFRASTRUCTURE **11**

A TOWNSCAPE PRESERVATION & ENHANCEMENT PLAN FOR NAVASOTA, TEXAS

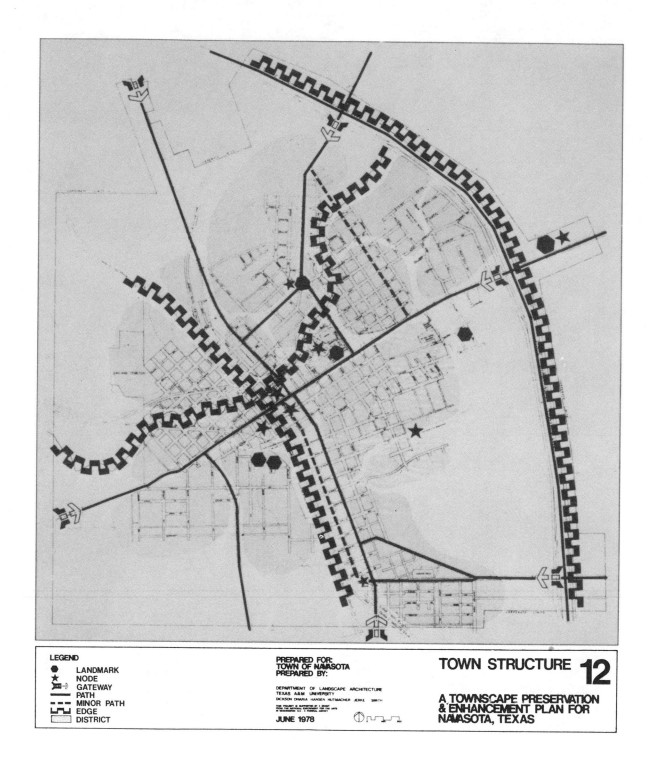

PREPARED FOR:
TOWN OF NAVASOTA
PREPARED BY:

DEPARTMENT OF LANDSCAPE ARCHITECTURE
TEXAS A&M UNIVERSITY
DICKSON DIMARIA HANSEN HUTTMACHER JERKE SMITH

THIS PROJECT IS SUPPORTED BY A GRANT
FROM THE NATIONAL ENDOWMENT FOR THE ARTS
IN WASHINGTON D.C. A FEDERAL AGENCY

JUNE 1978

TOWN STRUCTURE 12

A TOWNSCAPE PRESERVATION & ENHANCEMENT PLAN FOR NAVASOTA, TEXAS

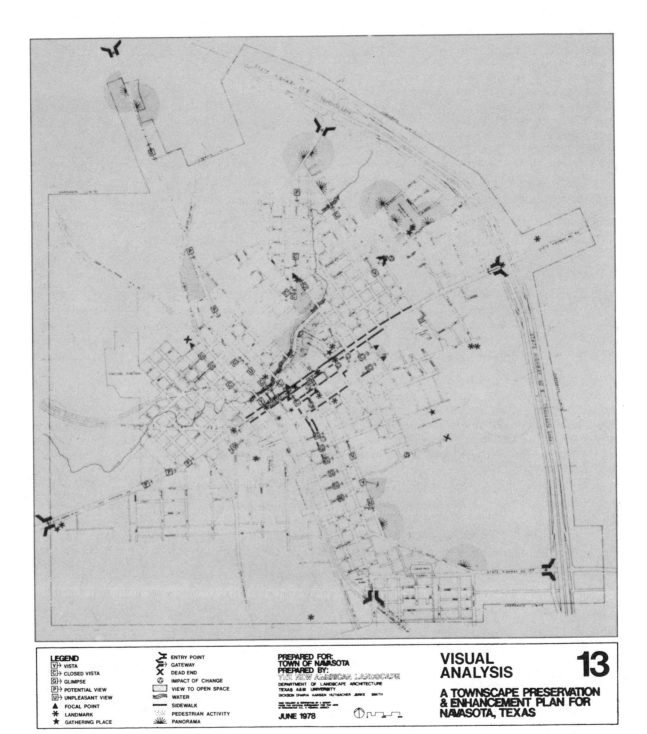

PREPARED FOR:
TOWN OF NAVASOTA
PREPARED BY:
THE NEW AMERICAN LANDSCAPE
DEPARTMENT OF LANDSCAPE ARCHITECTURE
TEXAS A&M UNIVERSITY
DICKSON DHARIA HANSEN HUTMACHER JERKE SMITH

THIS PROJECT IS SUPPORTED BY A GRANT
FROM THE NATIONAL ENDOWMENT FOR THE ARTS
IN WASHINGTON D.C. A FEDERAL AGENCY

JUNE 1978

VISUAL ANALYSIS   13

A TOWNSCAPE PRESERVATION & ENHANCEMENT PLAN FOR NAVASOTA, TEXAS

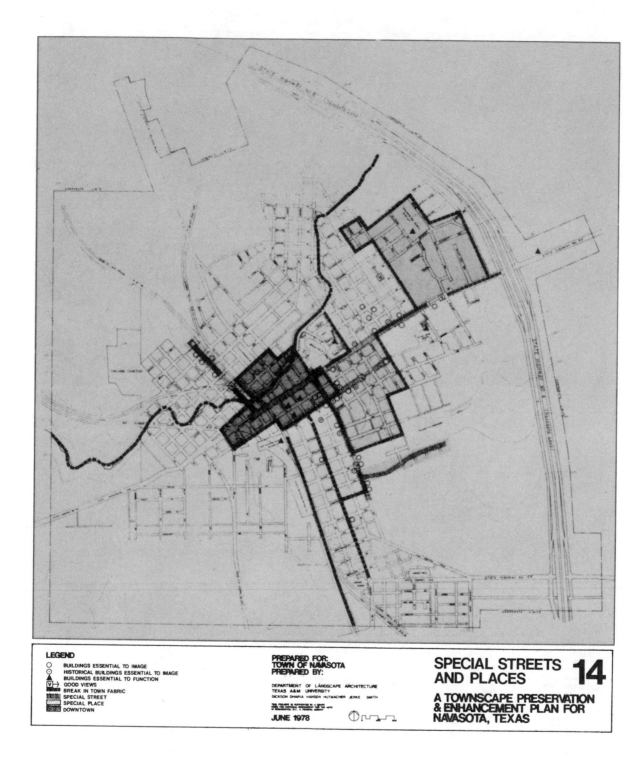

LEGEND
○ BUILDINGS ESSENTIAL TO IMAGE
⊙ HISTORICAL BUILDINGS ESSENTIAL TO IMAGE
▲ BUILDINGS ESSENTIAL TO FUNCTION
V→ GOOD VIEWS
⊞⊞ BREAK IN TOWN FABRIC
⬛ SPECIAL STREET
⬚ SPECIAL PLACE
⬛ DOWNTOWN

PREPARED FOR:
TOWN OF NAVASOTA
PREPARED BY:

DEPARTMENT OF LANDSCAPE ARCHITECTURE
TEXAS A&M UNIVERSITY
DICKSON DHARIA HANSEN HUTMACHER JERKE SMITH

JUNE 1978

SPECIAL STREETS
AND PLACES **14**

A TOWNSCAPE PRESERVATION
& ENHANCEMENT PLAN FOR
NAVASOTA, TEXAS

STEP FOUR — NAVASOTA UNIQUENESS PRESERVATION PLAN

This step will set forth the first major recommendation of the project, the creation of the *Navasota Uniqueness Preservation Plan* (N.U.P.)

This plan is the result of all the previous analysis and is a direct result of citizen opinion and the composite maps representing the natural, cultural and visual realms.

A. Composites

These composites represent the levels of uniqueness in Navasota in terms of these three areas of investigation and were combined to create the final map, the Navasota Uniqueness Preservation Plan.

The Natural Composite Map No. 15 — This map illustrates the natural areas of Navasota that significantly contribute to its overall town character and therefore should be preserved or enhanced. The three levels indicate the degree of natural appearance only. The areas most natural are those retaining surface water or heavy vegetation, as described on the density map. A moderately natural area contains some tree cover in addition to some groundcover. For example the creek zone is shown as most natural, while a typical neighborhood is moderately natural. All other areas support little or no vegetation, and do not significantly contribute to Navasota's natural character.

The Cultural Composite Map No. 16 — Overlaying all the cultural study maps resulted in a composite map. New areas were established according to different values and the influence man is having on the town's unique environment. Of particular value are the historic districts and the downtown commercial center. Navasota's downtown is the most unique cultural aspect to be preserved and enhanced. Every effort will be made in all aspects of this project to protect this important resource. The district of old homes is also a major cultural resource and has received the highest cultural uniqueness rating.

The Visual Composite Map No. 17 — The visual composite created three levels of value from the most to least importance to visual character. Areas not included in these designations are not necessarily of no visual character or of poor visual character. The intent of this composite is to identify those areas which are especially visually *unique* to Navasota. To this end, several areas of Navasota which are very pleasant and a justified source of pride are omitted from this map.

The following designations relate to the visual composite map.

Designation 1 (most important to visual character)
- Areasof high visual interest and uniqueness. This high level need not exist in every building or space but should characterize the entire area.
- The area should be recognized as special in the town.
- The area should have potential for further enhancement by the public or private sector.

Designation 2
- Area should be special in itself, but due to accessibility, surroundings, or undeveloped potential not be *as* special as designation 1.

Designation 3 (least important to visual character)
- Areas that are not currently enjoyed as special places but which have a high potential for future development.

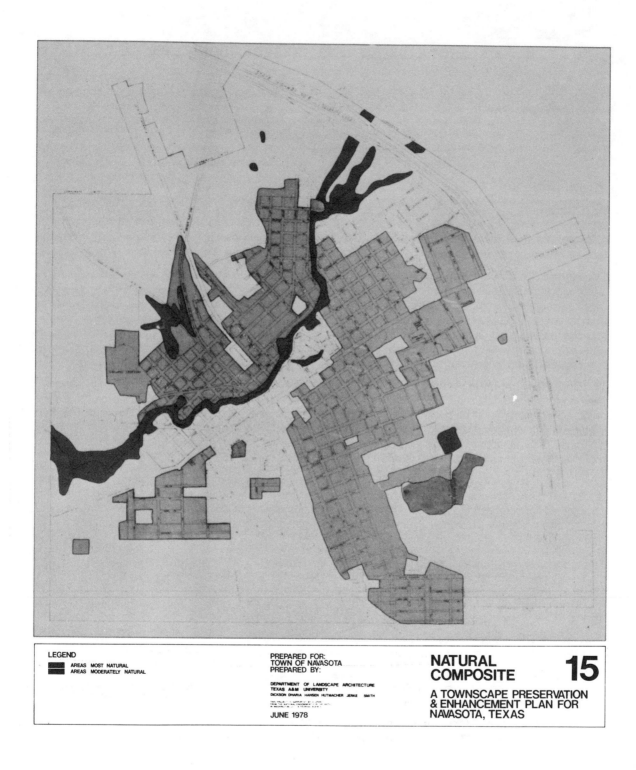

PREPARED FOR:
TOWN OF NAVASOTA
PREPARED BY:

DEPARTMENT OF LANDSCAPE ARCHITECTURE
TEXAS A&M UNIVERSITY
DICKSON DHARIA HANSEN HUTMACHER JERKE SMITH

THIS PROJECT IS SUPPORTED BY A GRANT
FROM THE NATIONAL ENDOWMENT FOR THE ARTS
IN WASHINGTON, D.C., A FEDERAL AGENCY

JUNE 1978

**NATURAL
COMPOSITE 15**

A TOWNSCAPE PRESERVATION
& ENHANCEMENT PLAN FOR
NAVASOTA, TEXAS

PREPARED FOR:
TOWN OF NAVASOTA
PREPARED BY:

DEPARTMENT OF LANDSCAPE ARCHITECTURE
TEXAS A&M UNIVERSITY
DICKSON DHARIA HANSEN HUTMACHER JEPKE SMITH

THIS PROJECT IS SUPPORTED BY A GRANT
FROM THE NATIONAL ENDOWMENT FOR THE ARTS
IN WASHINGTON D.C. A FEDERAL AGENCY

JUNE 1978

CULTURAL COMPOSITE   **16**

A TOWNSCAPE PRESERVATION
& ENHANCEMENT PLAN FOR
NAVASOTA, TEXAS

3.20 *Significant open space exists within the town.*

3.21 *Building details are important to town image.*

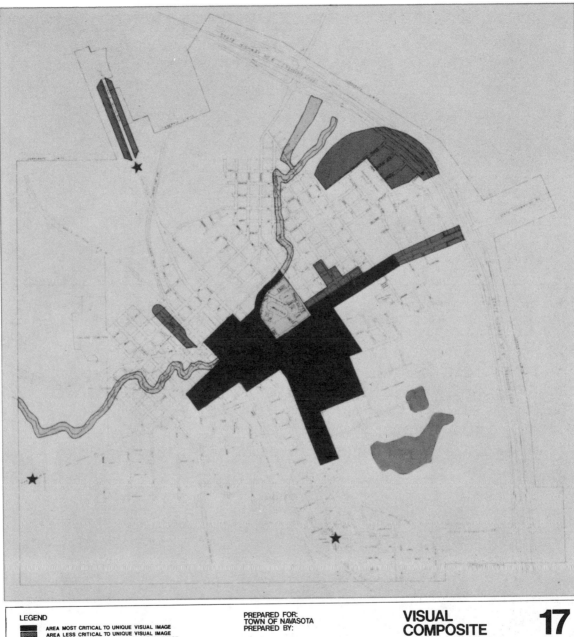

LEGEND
▓ AREA MOST CRITICAL TO UNIQUE VISUAL IMAGE
▒ AREA LESS CRITICAL TO UNIQUE VISUAL IMAGE
░ AREA LEAST CRITICAL TO UNIQUE VISUAL IMAGE
★ IMPORTANT ENTRANCES IN NEED OF DEFINITION

PREPARED FOR:
TOWN OF NAVASOTA
PREPARED BY:

DEPARTMENT OF LANDSCAPE ARCHITECTURE
TEXAS A&M UNIVERSITY
DICKSON DHARNA HANSEN KUTTMACHER JERKE SMITH

JUNE 1978

VISUAL COMPOSITE **17**

A TOWNSCAPE PRESERVATION
& ENHANCEMENT PLAN FOR
NAVASOTA, TEXAS

3.22 Light quality enhances many historic buildings.

B. The Navasota Uniqueness Preservation Plan (N.U.P.)

The map which becomes the N.U.P. is created using a direct overlay technique in which the three composite maps are superimposed and a fourth map is created. *See Map No. 18*. This map indicates those areas in Navasota which play a major role in the town's unique expression and should be preserved and enhanced as a major expression of official town policy. The essence of this plan is that it indicates the components of townscape uniqueness, identifies areas and aspects of town quality and places a relative value on them. This map allows the assigned areas of value to be located townwide and also allows the checking of previous maps to locate how the decision to give its value was made. This feature is very important because as values change, maps can be altered and the entire process remains alive and the plan is always a living useful document.

Three distinct uniqueness districts resulted from this composite process and they are shown on the NUP plan.

A. Areas indicated as the most critical are along parts of Cedar Creek and the most scenic, historic and vegetated portion of the southeast section of town.

B. Next in level is a larger potion of southeast Navasota which has fewer historic or scenic elements but is still very special.

C. The lowest level indicates the downtown area and the Washington Avenue entrance.

Taken all together these are the existing areas which illustrate what people think is special about Navasota. They are very general areas, however, the town ingredients which are found in them are what makes Navasota special and are those areas which need *specific policies for their preservation and enhancement*.

C. Recommendations

As its **first recommendation** this report would have the town of Navasota adopt this plan as its *Uniqueness Preservation Plan*. By doing this the town would set aside its special areas for carefully selected growth and change which would be designed to protect and enhance its image. The method for protecting these areas is the formation of a *Navasota Uniqueness Preservation Committee* (N.U.P.C.). The formation of this committee should be undertaken by city council and its organization and duties constitute this report's **second recommendation**. This committee should consist of a representative cross section of town's people who have been active in this project and who are willing to see its basic goals realized. The committee should be given the following duties, activities and powers:

1. The committee should have review power over *all* proposed growth and change in the special uniqueness districts indicated on the Navasota Uniqueness Preservation Plan. This will include both public and private development.

2. The committee should work closely with planning agencies and concerned citizens groups helping to coordinate all planning efforts which affect the uniqueness districts.

3. The committee should continually re-evaluate town goals and the values which went into the uniqueness plan. As a part of this activity the committee should hold workshops with citizens on a regular basis. The goals of these efforts will be to observe new growth and development and see that it is in keeping with town preservation goals and citizens values. If conflicts arise the committee should make recommendations for their resolution.

4. The committee should be given power to conduct special studies and suggest revisions to the areas indicated as special on the Navasota Uniqueness Preservation Plan.

5. The committee should be given power to establish evaluation guidelines based upon the special recommendations presented in Step Five, The Navasota Public Space Plan.

All recommendations made by the committee should go to city council for final action. It is further suggested that the committee number seven or nine persons and that length of service and compensation, if any, be determined by city council.

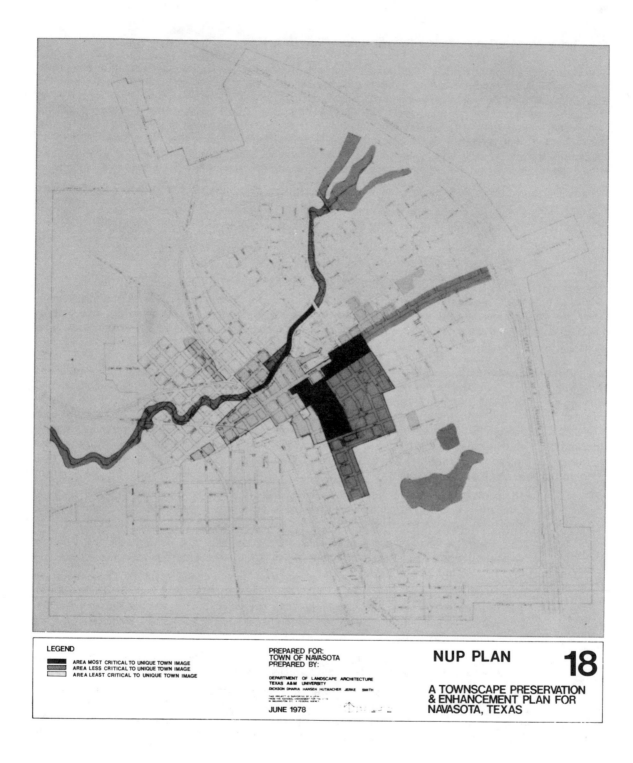

PREPARED FOR:
TOWN OF NAVASOTA
PREPARED BY:

DEPARTMENT OF LANDSCAPE ARCHITECTURE
TEXAS A&M UNIVERSITY
DICKSON DHARIA HANSEN HUTMACHER JERKE SMITH

THIS PROJECT IS SUPPORTED BY A GRANT
FROM THE NATIONAL ENDOWMENT FOR THE ARTS
IN WASHINGTON D.C. A FEDERAL AGENCY

JUNE 1978

NUP PLAN   18

A TOWNSCAPE PRESERVATION
& ENHANCEMENT PLAN FOR
NAVASOTA, TEXAS

The Next Step

The following Step Five will suggest a series of townwide polices for the orderly preservation and enhancement of Navasota's unique character. These policies will relate to the entire town, with specific recommendations for certain town zones which are *a direct outgrowth of the areas indicated on the Navasota Uniqueness Preservation Plan*. This step will deal specifically with the creation of a plan for Navasota's public areas and the preservation and enhancement of its public image. Until the policies suggested in Step Five can be incorporated into Navasota's comprehensive planning activities they should serve as guidelines in the *committee's evaluation of proposals for Navasota's unique area*.

The **third recommendation** of this report is that any development proposals in conflict with town goals for preservation should be denied by the N.U.P. Committee within these three uniqueness preservation zones of the *Navasota Uniqueness Preservation Plan*.

STEP FIVE — NAVASOTA PUBLIC SPACE PLAN

The Navasota Uniqueness Preservation Plan and its review arm the N.U.P. Committee will provide Navasota with basic direction for its preservation and enhancement activities. In this Step, however, we will also outline a more specific plan that is a direct outgrowth of the NUP plan and will help the citizens N.U.P. Committee make more specific decisions concerning Navasota's special areas and its townwide image. **This entire plan is Recommendation No. 4**.

Entitled the Conceptual *Public Space Plan,* it illustrates nine zones within Navasota which need special recommendations. (See Map No. 1A) These zones represent those areas which directly affect town quality and image and within which policy guidelines are needed. They are based upon a thorough analysis of Navasota and are indicated on the Conceptual Public Space Plan map.

A. Basic Guidelines

These guidelines should be central to all future town growth and change decisions as they affect the protection and enhancement of town quality.

- A townwide effort must be made to protect identified town uniqueness and enhance those areas needing improvement.
- All growth decisions and plans for new construction should reflect the desire to produce a town of high quality and character.
- Citizens should be involved in an organized way in all town growth and change decisions which affect town quality.
- The public areas should receive the highest quality of planning and design and reflect the desires of the people for a high public standard of living.
- The overriding goal should be to preserve character, spirit, quality and image· which are essential to Navasota's sense of place. And finally,
- A townwide street-tree ordinance including a policy on cutting, planting and types should be enacted. This ordinance should require private developers to plant trees in their developments in keeping with a long range town street tree planting program.

B. Specific Guidelines by Zone

The following list of specific recommendations, by zone, illustrate the townwide recommendations suggested by this report.

Quad Parks — Zone 1

The four neighborhood, or quad, parks are designed to put local residents within walking or bike riding distance of recreational and natural features which are shared and enjoyed at the community level. Each park is linked to the other features of Navasota's Public Space Plan. Though the parks are designed primarily for local use, each park should have distinctive features that may attract use at the townwide level.

- The name of the park should reinforce its unique features and/or should give a locational clue.
- The parks should emphasize access by foot or bicycle, as well as by car.
- The parks would provide both natural and recreational opportunities.

Entrance Zones 2, 3, 4,

The entrance to town gives its first impression to residents and visitors alike. These recommendations are designed to *preserve* or *enhance* the major entrances to Navasota.

Covered here will be the west entrance (from Washington on the Brazos), the north entrance (from Bryan) and the south entrance (from Hempstead and Conroe) and the crossroads. The entrance from Anderson will be described under the special district zone.

South Entrance — Zone 2

The south entrance from Hempstead and Houston, is like other entrances in that one progresses from a rural environment to an urban environment, but unlike the others this entrance has a particular point which triggers a sense of entry — the Carver School and railroad tracks. The recommendations to reinforce this entrance include these:

- Sign the entrance to welcome the visitor to Navasota.
- Develop the Carver School for a community facility.
- Encourage residential development south of Teague Street, commercial to the north.
- Plants, street trees and structures like fences should be used to screen residential development.
- Signs, light, awnings, etc. should be controlled by policy.
- The quality of new development should be in keeping with positive town image and seek to avoid bright colors or distracting shapes.

North Entrance — Zone 3

The north entrance, from Bryan, is a long "rural experience" that disolves into the commercial outskirts of downtown at Northside Street. The commercial area is chaotic as it exists now — the telephone and electrical wires, the signs and flashing lights and lack of organization of commercial development and parking all detract from an otherwise pleasant experience. These recommendations would help remedy this situation:

- The existing natural conditions north of Northside Drive should be maintained.
- Establish an entry point at the curve in the road near Northside Drive by widening the road, installing a welcome sign and putting in a median strip.
- Utilities should go underground south of Northside Drive.
- The rural interest should be maintained by the maintenance and organization of the machinery dealer's displays.
- A sign ordinance should be enacted to control sign size and configuration.
- Curbs should be installed south of Northside Drive and planting used to screen parking adjacent to commercial enterprises.
- Crossing the creek should be an event that indicated an entrance to downtown. This can be accomplished with signage and good design on either side of the bridge.

3.23 *Many historic homes line major streets.*

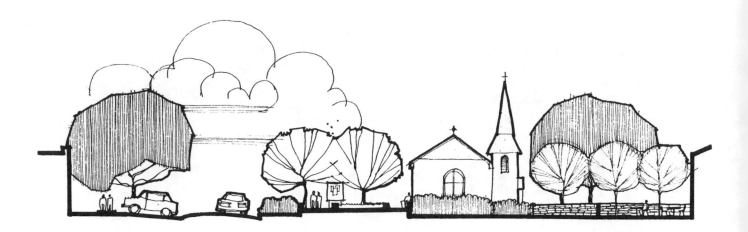

West Entrance — Zone 4

The west entrance, from Brenham, is probably one of the least defined entrances to Navasota. The initial image is very positive because the road passes by the very pleasant Brule Park and VFW Hall. However, there is no indication to visitors that this is Navasota. Furthermore, after the VFW Hall, Washington Street soon becomes a rather disjointed mixture of commercial and residential structures distracting from the initial positive image.

> Guidelines:
>
> * Require that all new structures meet designated appearance and signing standards and encourage existing development to do the same.
> * Retain a mix of commercial and residential uses, i.e. — do not create a commercial "strip."
> * Require that large retail sales building remain close to downtown — no further west than the existing lumber yards.
> * Retain the deep lot situation along the street, and encourage a variety of set-backs.
> * Create sidewalks and eventually a bike lane to the VFW Hall.
> * Place a permanent "Welcome to Navasota" sign in conjunction with a VFW Hall.

The Crossroads — The Intersection of Washington & LaSalle

The intersection of Highway 6 and Washington Street creates a very important point of orientation for both the residents of Navasota and visitors to the town. The traffic problems relating to this location will be discussed in the "Downtown Zone" section, but these recommendations are offered to help make the crossroads a more definite focal point in the center of town.

> * Sign at or just before the crossroads clarifying direction, destinations, road numbers, etc.
> * Design a mosiac pattern at the crossroads to accentuate the crossroads.
> * Put all utilities underground.

Special District — Zone 5 High Priority Zone

The special district includes the majority of those areas in Navasota mentioned on questionnaires and during interviews with Navasota people. Much of the positive image and character is within this area of the community. The area is characterized by fine historic structures, mature vegetation, well kept homes and churches, sidewalks, flowers, wood and brick and stone construction. A number of homes are undergoing renovation and some new construction is being undertaken. The following guidelines are suggested for this zone:

> * New construction in this area should be in harmony with the existing image character of the older town fabric.
> * A special district ordinance should be designed to guide all future change in this zone.
> * Commercial incursions should be very selective, and existing commercial development should be modified or relocated to fit the desired image.

- Tree replanting from a recommended list should be undertaken with special emphasis upon the entrance from the by-pass to downtown (see suggested Tree Matrix).
- A park should be created on the open land in front of the Lutheran Church and the existing commercial structure should be modified or relocated.
- New uses should be sought for older homes along Washington when these structures become vacant.
- New development at the by-pass and Washington should be in keeping with street image and town policy concerning by-pass development.
- The view from Washington Avenue to the Presbyterian Church should remain open.
- The use of McAlphine Street as a one-way street within this zone should not occur without careful study as to neighborhood impact.
- The District should be placed on the National Register of Historic Place as a Historic District.

Downtown District — Zone 6 High Priority Zone

Navasota's downtown district is its finest zone next to the potential special district. Here the mixture of fine old commercial buildings and a busy shopping area create for Navasota what many Texas cities are trying to regain at great expense — *a vital downtown*. The major town goal for this zone is to protect this *unique resource*. Recommendations for this zone include:

- The creation of a public gathering and sitting place, in particular between Cedar Creek and Washington Avenue and the end of Farquar Street as it intersects with Washington Avenue should be a high priority.
- The continued revitalization of Railroad Avenue with the creation of public outdoor spaces. New building use should recognize the various cultural groups using this unique section of downtown.
- Building facades should undergo selective renovation toward a common plan. Each individual building owner should be consulted often during this process.
- Major street planting is required to give this area shade, visual interest and a sense of place compatible with other portions of downtown.
- The new City Hall Annex should be revitalized and public space provided in association with it.
- Zoning for downtown should allow for activities other than commercial in recycled buildings (such as housing on upper floors).
- New activities such as restaurants and hotels should be encouraged.
- A coordinated system of street hardware, such as lights, benches, mail boxes, paving and trash recepticles should be designed.
- Standards of signs should be developed.
- A long range plan for underground utilities installation should be implemented.
- Off street parking should be developed in well landscaped lots.
- Parking should be reorganized, with new lots provided, and circulation along Washington Avenue should be improved.
- Conversion of alley ways to pedestrian circulation with limited access to service vehicles.
- Creation of strong sense of entry to downtown area including a feature at the historical crossroads.
- The use of compatible materials and building bulk and height for new downtown construction.
- The creation of a historical theme park in association with the old cottonseed oil mill.
- Conduct a revitalization of Cedar Creek in the "downtown area" — that part of the creek between 10th and Brosig.
- This district should be evaluated for inclusion on the National Register of Historic places as an Historic District.

3.25 **WASHINGTON STREET**

3.26 **ZONE 6**

CAFE

3.27 **ZONE 6**

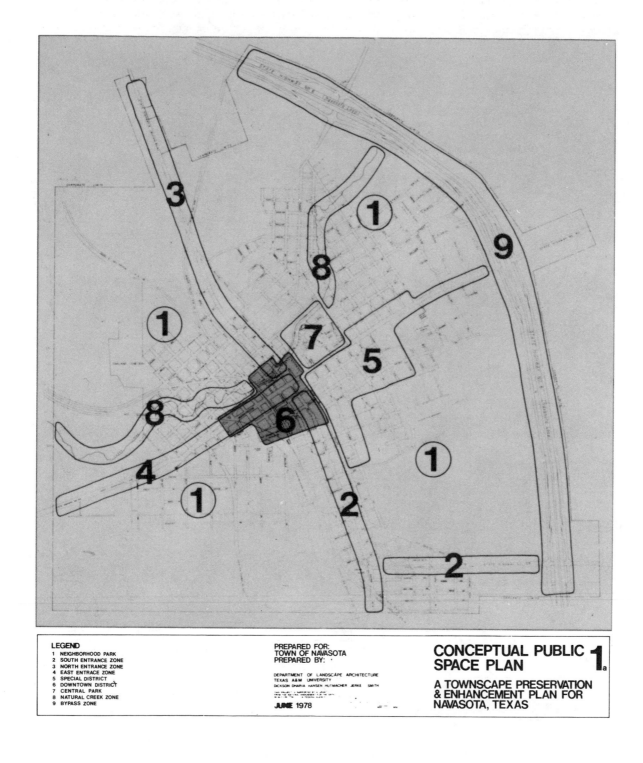

Public Space — Zone 7

The public space at the Brule Field complex is presently primarily a school oriented space which excludes many citizens and visitors not interested in school activities. The central location of the site on Washington Avenue and proximity to downtown suggests that better use of this land for public activities would provide Navasota citizens with a centrally located space for school and public activities and tourists. Four major user groups will influence the design of such a space. The school users, the commercial users, the neighborhood users and the visitors and general public using Washington Avenue. The following is a description of potential recommendations for use areas in this space.

- Park design should enhance Washington Avenue, solve circulation problems, provide seating areas for students, improve play areas, provide pick-up area for school busses.
- It should create an activity space with a focal point along Washington Avenue. A lake is suggested.
- The provision for pedestrian circulation/bicycle circulation throughout the park is essential.
- The park should provide restrooms and perhaps concessions.
- The park should be connected to the creek.
- The swimming area should be redesigned to become a more imaginative public space.
- The car lot adjacent to the park should be relocated and the land used to tie Washington Avenue to the park, visually and physically.

The Creek — Zone 8

Cedar Creek has been recognized by many Navasota people as a potential positive element in terms of town image. This study also concluded that with work and creative thought the Creek could become the major feature in Navasota. To that end, recommendations are made for three sections of the Creek: "*Downtown*" the area from 10th to Brosig, which is covered in the downtown district and the central park district, "*North Creek*" from Brosig to the Highway 6 by-pass and "*South Creek*" from 10th Street beyond 3rd Street to the City Limits. General recommendations for North and South Creek include:

- The introduction of water from upstream to insure regular water flow — perhaps with a windmill.
- A master planting scheme for its entire length.
- Improved public access and the creation of public areas along its banks.
- A dam should be constructed to produce a pool and waterfall feature.
- A regular maintenance program should be implemented once the creek is cleaned and cleared of brush and while the longer range plans are being implemented.
- A continuous pedestrian walkway and bike path should run from 3rd Street to the Highway 6 by-pass.
- Wildlife should be encouraged.
- Redevelopment should be as natural as possible, however public safety may require some wall, improved creek bed handrails and pedestrian bridges.

The By-Pass — Zone 9

Until recently the growth in Navasota has been compact and inward-focused, creating a strong and busy downtown, a ring of residential development and an agricultural setting. Today's existence of Highway 6 and the rapid growth of the city have set a scene that could undermine both the appearance of the town and the vitality of downtown by encouraging growth, especially commercial growth, along the by-pass. In order to prevent this, these recommendations are offered to help Navasota retain its character and still accommodate development.

- Land north of the proposed northeast park should remain as open space or agriculture.
- The area on the town side of the by-pass at the intersection of Washington and the by-pass should be allowed to develop commercially. The choice of development type is very important to assure that it does not draw people away from downtown. A hotel or motel, restaurant, amusement area, office building, or similar service-oriented activity would be best.
- The remaining areas inside the by-pass would be best used for residential development. Some selected tourist/traveler businesses (gas stations, cafes) might be permitted south of Washington Avenue, but each's size, signing, and design should be carefully scrutinized.
- Design standards should be established, especially for commercial buildings.
- No structure should be placed on the crest of high areas as this makes them particularly predominant.

3.28 **NATURAL AREA**

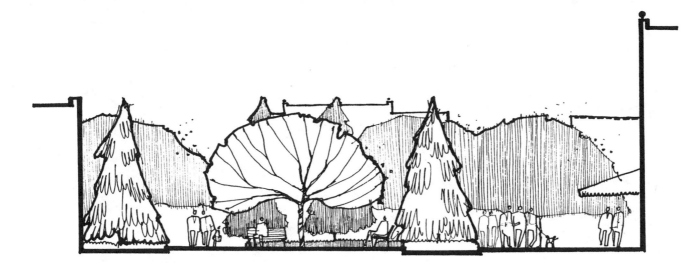

3.29 **SITTING AREA**

C. Priorities

Map No 2A indicates three priority levels in terms of implementation phasing. These priorities are not tied to specific time periods because Navasota officials must decide the level of expenditures to commit each year and what levels of improvements to require from the private sector. Very specific detailed suggestions are also included here to further indicate the level of design which might be done in the priority levels.

D. Detailed Design Studies

To further expand the ideas indicated in the *Conceptual Public Space Plan* a series of detailed design studies were conducted. Those areas selected for design and their specific suggestions are as follows:

LaSalle Park — Proposed park in front of the Presbyterian Chruch on McAlpine Street. Two design ideas are expressed: Map 4, showing the retention of the existing gas station; and Map 3, showing the removal of the gas station. These designs are characterized by:

- A large open green space
- The creation of a major view from Washington Avenue to the church steeple.
- New tree and shrub planting
- Places to sit, talk, eat lunch and relax
- New sidewalks and plaza areas
- A small pool and fountain shown on Map 3

Washington Avenue — Washington Avenue between the railroad tracks and the crossroads. This high priority downtown area is the major focal point of downtown improvements. The goal was to create a major public area improvement plan which gives focus to Navasota's unique and active downtown district. Major aspects of this design include:

- Improved on street parking and the creation of extra traffic lanes
- Extensive street tree planting
- Pedestrian areas free of auto traffic
- Places to sit, talk and relax in the sun or shade
- New paving and crosswalks
- Public conveniences like night lighting, water fountains, telephones, mail drops and trash receptables.
- Awnings to provide sun and rain protection
- Outdoor cafes
- Improved traffic flow
- A new plaza at the foot of Farquhar Street designed for sitting, eating, outdoor exhibits, noontime music shows, shade, a place to meet friends or read the news
- Building facade improvement suggestions

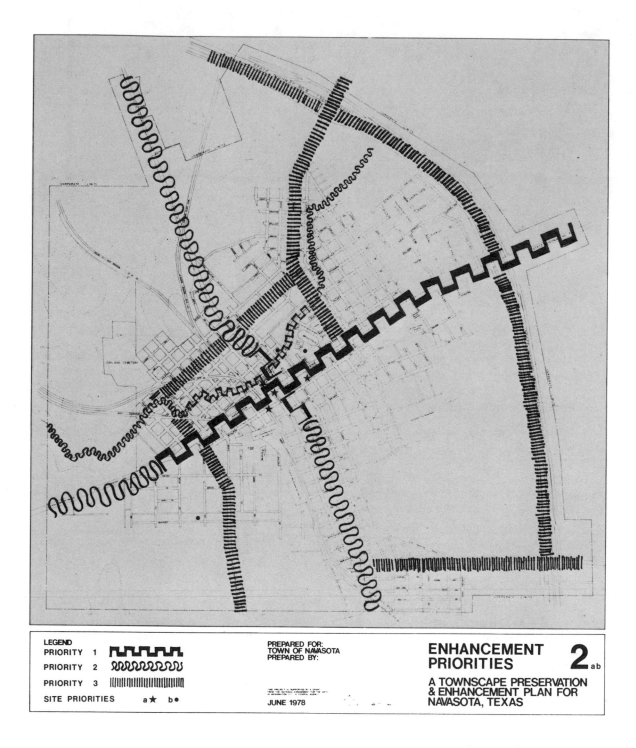

LEGEND
PRIORITY 1
PRIORITY 2
PRIORITY 3
SITE PRIORITIES   a ★   b ●

PREPARED FOR:
TOWN OF NAVASOTA
PREPARED BY:

JUNE 1978

ENHANCEMENT
PRIORITIES   2ab

A TOWNSCAPE PRESERVATION
& ENHANCEMENT PLAN FOR
NAVASOTA, TEXAS

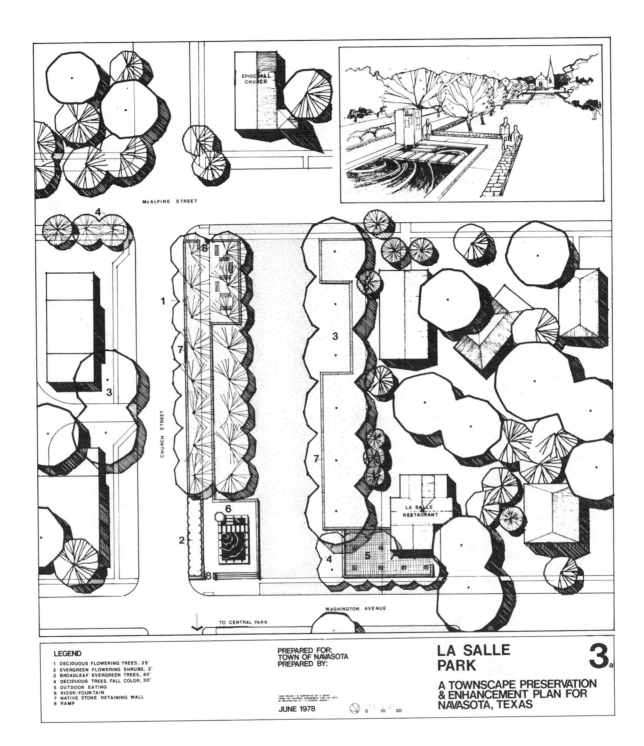

EPISCOPAL CHURCH

McALPINE STREET

CHURCH STREET

LA SALLE RESTAURANT

WASHINGTON AVENUE

TO CENTRAL PARK

LEGEND

1 DECIDUOUS FLOWERING TREES. 25'
2 EVERGREEN FLOWERING SHRUBS. 3'
3 BROADLEAF EVERGREEN TREES. 40'
4 DECIDUOUS TREES. FALL COLOR, 30'
5 OUTDOOR EATING
6 KIOSK/FOUNTAIN
7 NATIVE STONE RETAINING WALL
8 RAMP

PREPARED FOR:
TOWN OF NAVASOTA
PREPARED BY:

THIS PROJECT IS SUPPORTED BY A GRANT
FROM THE NATIONAL ENDOWMENT FOR THE ARTS
IN WASHINGTON D.C. A FEDERAL AGENCY

JUNE 1978

0   10   20

LA SALLE PARK

3ₐ

A TOWNSCAPE PRESERVATION
& ENHANCEMENT PLAN FOR
NAVASOTA, TEXAS

3.30 **HISTORIC VIEW AND POTENTIAL PARK**   **ZONE 6**

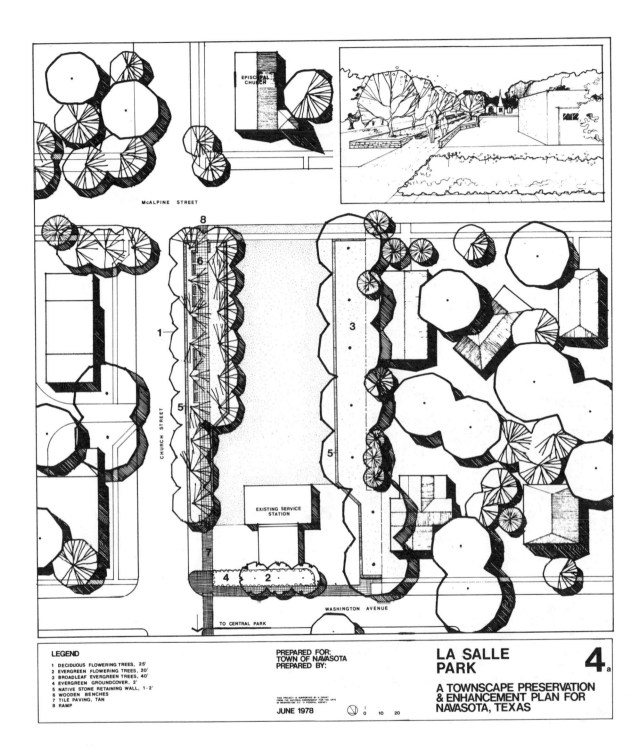

McALPINE STREET

EPISCOPAL CHURCH

8

6

1

5

CHURCH STREET

3

5

EXISTING SERVICE STATION

7

4 2

TO CENTRAL PARK

WASHINGTON AVENUE

LEGEND

1 DECIDUOUS FLOWERING TREES, 25'
2 EVERGREEN FLOWERING TREES, 20'
3 BROADLEAF EVERGREEN TREES, 40'
4 EVERGREEN GROUNDCOVER, 2'
5 NATIVE STONE RETAINING WALL, 1 - 2'
6 WOODEN BENCHES
7 TILE PAVING, TAN
8 RAMP

PREPARED FOR:
TOWN OF NAVASOTA
PREPARED BY:

THIS PROJECT IS SUPPORTED BY A GRANT
FROM THE NATIONAL ENDOWMENT FOR THE ARTS
IN WASHINGTON D.C. A FEDERAL AGENCY.

JUNE 1978

0   10   20

LA SALLE PARK

4a

A TOWNSCAPE PRESERVATION
& ENHANCEMENT PLAN FOR
NAVASOTA, TEXAS

3.31 **DOWNTOWN NAVASOTA**

Railroad Avenue — Railroad Avenue from Washington Avenue to Holland Street represents a unique opportunity for Navasota. This outdoor space and the historic business along its edge could become the focal point of building restoration. The design suggestions in this report should happen in several phases and will depend upon future trends in land use, will new buildings be built in downtown? And transportation, will Amtrak from Dallas to Houston stop in Navasota? Looking toward the future and at the present the design suggests:

- Extensive tree planting to provide shade and visual interest
- Re-organizing parking
- Pedestrian sitting areas, plazas, and conveniences
- Additional building restoration such as the Smith Hotel
- The potential for an Amtrak and bus station with a restaurant made from old railroad dining cars.
- Display booths, fountains, information kiosks and lighting
- The potential closing of McAlpine Street to create a major pedestrian space

City Hall Annex — Navasota's need for new city space was met by the purchase of the old Gulf States Building. The design sugestions represent a concept based upon a desire to:

- Organize parking for public convenience
- Provide space outdoors for people to sit, wait for friends, eat lunch, fill out forms, and relax
- Provide shade and visual relief with extensive tree planting
- Create a positive image for the new facility
- Encourage new private construction in the area by becoming an attractive and active civil focal point

The "Plaza" — A central place for Navasota's citizens enjoyment and for Navasota's central business district's health and revitalization. The characteristics of this design are:

- A pedestrian counterpoise to the auto oriented Washington Avenue
- Providing a "soft," shaded place for pedestrians in Navasota's central business district
- Organization of existing auto parking and loading zones
- Revival of the unique, former economic heart of Navasota, The Cotton Seed Oil Mill, by transforming the area into "Pioneer Village" market places
- Meshing of the built-up business district and the naturally meandering Cedar Creek Park producing a structured, outdoor, citizen's arena for activities (i.e., City Amphitheater focused on creek, shore, and island, the Pavilion for sack lunch gatherings, the Plaza for a dignified city statement defining "The Center")
- Creation of a unique experience which will strengthen the central business district's draw of people yet not disrupt the already healthy flow of auto traffic which interfaces with the businesses on Washington Avenue

Central Park — The old Navasota high school site is suggested to become a major central park for Navasota's citizens. Its extensive public land and walking distance from all parts of town, fine old trees, public visiblity and relationship to Cedar Creek make it an excellent place for this activity. Recommendations include:

- A new little league park
- A small lake for toy boats and ducks. An extensive series of special areas for sitting, eating lunch, watching water, hearing music and walking
- A fountain and lunch area
- An information center for tourists
- Extensive open lawns and tree planting
- Concession stand and public restrooms
- Extensive development of pedestrian areas along Cedar Creek and pedestrian access from park to creek
- Creative playgrounds
- A band shelter for music concerts and political rallies
- Extensive use of flowering trees
- Free and spontaneous areas for individual choice of leisure activities

3.32 **RESIDENTIAL STREET**

E. Street Tree Planting Program

The major effort the city can undertake is a tree planting program for the streets and public areas. While this report did not undertake a detailed tree inventory and did not undertake the design of a comprehensive street tree plan, it did recognize the importance of trees to Navasota's image. As part of **Recommendation Number Four** Navasota should undertake an extensive tree planting program. The areas indicated as high priority on Map 2AB, enhancement priorities, are where the planting should begin. It should continue over a long period of time. The following tree matrix indicates the types of trees which seem best suited to Navasota and are recommended for tree planting programs. See Map 2AB Enhancement Priorities.

TREE MATRIX

	SCIENTIFIC NAME	COMMON NAME	LIFE EXPECTANCY			GROWTH RATE			MATURE FORM				SOIL TOLERANCE				PEST RESISTANCE	EVERGREEN	ATTRACTIVE FLOWER OR FOLIAGE	GOOD FALL COLOR
			Short	Medium	Long	Slow	Medium	Fast	Pyramidal	Columnar	Rounded	Horizontal Branching	Acid	Dry	Wet	All Types				
SMALL TREES 20'-35'	Cornus Florida	Flowering Dogwood		•		•						•	•						•	•
	Cercis Canadensis	Eastern Redbud		•		•					•					•			•	
	Koelretaria Paniculata	Rain Tree		•			•				•			•					•	
	Lagerstroemia Indica	Crape Myrtle		•		•					•					•			•	
	Malus Spp.	Flowering Crabapple		•		•					•					•			•	•
	Prunus Mexicana	Mexican Plum		•		•					•					•			•	
MEDIUM TREES 35'-65'	Gleditsia Triacanthos	Thornless Honey Locust		•							•					•			•	
	Liquidambar Styraciflua	Sweet Gum			•	•			•							•	•			•
	Magnolia Grandiflora	Southern Magnolia			•	•			•					•				•	•	
	Quercus Virginiana	Live Oak			•	•					•					•	•	•		•
	Pistacia Chinesis	Chinese Pistache	•				•				•					•				
TALL TREES 65'-up	Carya Illinoensis	Pecan		•		•					•					•				
	Fraxinus Americana	White Ash		•		•					•				•					•
	Platamus Occidentalis	Sycamore	•					•			•				•					
	Quercus Macrocarpa	Bur Oak		•	•						•	•		•						•
	Quercus Nigra	Water Oak		•		•				•					•				•	•
	Quercus Phellos	Willow Oak		•		•					•					•			•	•
	Sapium Sebiferum	Chinese Tallow Tree	•					•			•					•			•	•
	Ulmas Crassifolia	Cedar Elm		•	•					•			•						•	•
	Taxodium Distchum	Bald Cypress	•			•			•					•					•	•
	Pinus Caribaea	Slash Pine	•				•		•						•			•		•
	Pinus Taeda	Loblolly Pine		•			•		•						•			•		•

STEP SIX — IMPLEMENTATION

The two key aspects of the Navasota Preservation and Enhancement Program are: 1) *The Navasota Uniqueness Preservation Plan* and its companion, the *Navasota Uniqueness Preservation Committee*; and, 2) The *Conceptual Public Space Plan*. Each of these major components of the overall *Navasota Preservation and Enhancement Program* has its own individual implementation aspects. The most desirable goal is for the town of Navasota to incorporate the *Navasota Preservation and Enhancement Program* into its townwide comprehensive plan and zoning ordinance. The action would balance preservation and enhancement needs with the needs for housing, industrial development, utilities, transportation, recreation and commercial development, and become a policy guideline for future town growth and change. Until this is done, however, certain aspects of the *Preservation and Enhancement Program* may be implemented by the town using various implementation tools which are available or which can be created. These tools fall into the following categories and will be discussed as they relate to the two major program components.

Implementation A — The Navasota Uniqueness Preservation Plan

This plan, as presented in Step 4, is designed to locate and protect Navasota's unique areas. Most of its implementation will fall within the legislative and administrative category and is dependent upon:

- Adoption of the plan by city council as official town policy.
- The creation of the Navasota Uniqueness Preservation Committee and the granting of the powers outlined in Step 4.
- The directing of existing town policy toward its objectives and the creation of new town policies designed to achieve its goals.
- The creation of a positive attitude vis-a-vis the preservation of uniqueness through public town meetings.

The **public programs** sector will play a limited role in this plan but might include such things as including qualified buildings or districts on the state or national register of historic places. Most of the qualified buildings will be located in one of the three uniqueness districts. The National Park Service and the Texas Historical Commission will provide counseling to communities in this area of activity.

Private enterprise can and should play a major role in the implementation of this portion of the plan. The major role it plays is to become informed concerning town preservation policy and design proposed developments in harmony with stated town goals. Resulting from this activity would be a better private investment and a better town image which is conducive to long term project financial success. In this manner much town improvement can occur as part of the normal development process.

Implementation B — The Conceptual Public Space Plan

The Public Space Plan is a conceptual physical plan requiring design and implementation as a portion of town improvement. The suggestions, if accepted, should be made a part of each year's capital improvement budget and implemented in phases with the highest priority areas receiving immediate attention.

Legislative and administrative actions required here include:

- The selection by city officials of projects to be undertaken within the nine zones of the public space plan, and the establishment of project priorities.
- A commitment by town officials to the improvement of public areas as part of each year's capital improvements budget.
- The willingness of the town to conduct detailed design studies of the priority areas.

Public programs and funding sources can be very useful in project implementation. However town officials must choose which programs best suit current town needs. Some programs which might prove useful are:

Federal Programs

> *Watershed Protection and Flood Protection Prevention — Small Watersheds*: Administered by the Soil Conservation Service (Department of Agriculture) to provide grants for planning, designing and installing projects on rivers and creeks. One applicable use for this aid is in the development of recreational and civic projects.

> *Small Reclamation Projects*: Administered by the Bureau of Reclamation (Department of Interior). Fully reimbursible loans and grants for rehabilitation, betterment, or construction of water resource developments.

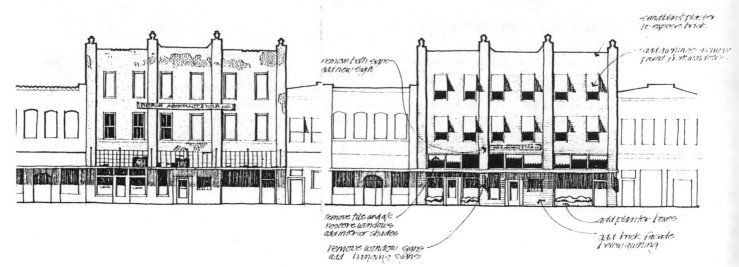

3.33 Facade improvements

Outdoor Recreation — Aquisition, Development and Planning (*Land and Water Conservation Fund Grants*): Administered by the Heritage Conservation and Recreation Service in the Department of the Interior. This fund provides grants for a whole range of outdoor recreation projects.

Community Development Block Grants: Administered by the Community Planning and Development branch of the Department of Housing and Urban Development. Navasota qualifies for "discretionary grant" money, which would be distributed by the city, reflecting its established priority.

Housing Rehabilitation Loans: Administered by the Community Planning and Development branch of the Department of Housing and Urban Development. If the housing units qualify under HUD rules, they may be eligible for federal loans.

State Programs

The *State Highway Department* offer "PL-112" money to committees to do planning studies. These studies tend to be transportation oriented but this is not a requirement.

Most housing rehabilitation, recreational development and similar grants are sponsored by the Federal government, who uses the State as a clearing house.

Local Programs & Tools

Zoning: Especially important to note is that the State of Texas provides for the establishment of Historic Districts, where special regulations can be used to preserve character.

Subdivision Regulations and Design Standards: These tools can assure that new development in the community will be of high quality and will suitably supplement and enhance existing structures and spaces.

Transportation Plans, *Housing Plans and other specialized documents* establish town policy in the realm of these more specific topics. Well-done documents of this sort greatly aid in consistently high-quality decisions on the part of town officials.

Private Sector

The private sector can do a major job at this stage by doing new development of high quality, not just in the uniqueness zones, but townwide. One increasingly popular tool being used by many cities and towns is the *special district* or *downtown development district*. Navasota businessmen may want to explore this option and determine if this is a desired direction for them to encourage city officials to pursue. The downtown development district can assume broad powers and undertake, working in concert with town officials and citizens; planning administration, street improvements, activity places such as plazas and malls, promotional work, transportation improvements, urban art and beautification projects, provide downtown operations such as museums and auditoriums. A complete analysis of this option is available from The Downtown Research Development Center, 270 Madison Ave., New York, N.Y., 10016.

Other items include:
- The assistance of service clubs in the implementation of tree planting or similar projects.
- Voluntary compliance with such items as sign control, tree planting, parking lot screening, building rehabilitation and creating public amenities.

The key to all implementation efforts is for the town to decide which parts of the **Navasota Uniqueness Preservation Plan** and the **Conceptual Public Space Plan** it wants to implement, and then seek out the *programs*, *tools*, and *techniques* which best solve the implementation needs.

One final note is that the town should implement some projects within six months to one year to provide incentive for continued citizen interest and participation. Other implementation should continue on a medium and long range basis as funds and priorities permit.

STEP SEVEN — MONITOR & UPDATE

The last phase of the process deals with the evaluation of what is being implemented. This step is very critical. **Recommendation Five** is that it be the major long term activity of the *Navasota Uniqueness Preservation Committee*. As aspects of the plan are implemented, and the impacts of revised town policies are noticeable within the town, evaluation of results must occur. The range of these evaluations should be comprehensive and extend from the townwide scale of planning activities to whether or not a new bench on Washington Avenue is comfortable. While no strict guidelines will be offered, as flexibility in approach will better reflect the changing nature of Navasota and the committee, certain questions are offered here as suggestions to future committees undertaking evaluation. Those persons undertaking evaluation should ask:

1. Is the spirit of the plan being reinforced by town policy?
2. Are the results of plan policies producing the level of preservation and enhancement desired by Navasota? If not, what changes need to be made in the planning process?
3. Are the values of the citizens reflected in the implementation of plan recommendations? If not how can more citizens be involved.
4. Have the plan's policies protected the unique and special areas identified during the character map and town uniqueness plan process?
5. Do the public spaces implemented during the Public Space Plan activities serve people's needs? Are they used? By whom? Do they need alteration?
6. What lessons can be learned which will allow alteration of future projects before they are built?
7. How well is the townwide street tree plan doing? Are the suggested trees surviving? Are older trees being maintained and protected?
8. Is new development in keeping with town image goals?
9. Are any enforcement ordinances required to protect certain areas? Would voluntary compliance serve just as well if town policies were made more explicit?
10. Has the general quality of town life been improved? Could it be better with revisions to the preservation and enhancement plan or the implementation process?

The answers to these and similar questions should provide guidance for revisions to the planning process, revisions to the values which created the composites which created the town uniqueness plan and revisions to town policy where required. If this monitor and update phase is carried out and its evaluation results are fed into the process wheel, the Navasota Preservation and Enhancement Plan can always remain flexible and relevant to the needs of Navasota's people.

CONCLUSION

The material included in this report represents many hours of effort by the study team and the citizens and public officials of Navasota. Central to the plan's goal, a Navasota which preserves its unique attributes and is enhanced by proper new development, is that the values which created the plan were drawn from the people and not imposed from without. During the entire process the questions "Is it true to Navasota?" and "Can the quality of the town's Public space and image be retained or enhanced in keeping with people's values?" served as a frame of reference to the study team's progress. The process designed as part of this project is flexible, as is the final plan. In fact the plan is never really final but should be an ongoing activity which can change as values change and thus remain fresh with use.

The citizens of Navasota and their elected officials hopefully will study the plan, find its ideas sound and proceed to implement its recommendations. If, however, certain aspects are not thought sound they should be revised within the process and new recommendations should be created. In no case should the people be kept out of this process as it is a plan for their future as well as the future image of Navasota.

Thomas Jefferson spoke to this idea during the early days of our republic:

"I know no safe depository of the ultimate powers of the society but the people themselves; and if we think them not enlightened enough to exercise their control with a wholesome discretion, the remedy is not to take it from them, but to inform their discretion."

Thomas Jefferson, 1820

3.34 *Older homes have become shops and restaurants.*

3.35 *Downtown remains active and successful.*

end notes

[1] Johnson, R., May 8, 1984. "Iowa Villages' Tourism Boom Brings Questionable Progress," *The Wall Street Journal.* New York.

[2] Blundell, W., July 3, 1984. "New Rural Migration Overburdens and Alters Once-Sleepy Hamlets," *The Wall Street Journal.* New York.
(Editorial), September 1, 1980. "Small Town USA: Growing and Growning." *Time.* New York: Time, Inc.
(Editorial), August 5, 1984. "Village is Tough on Developer," *Houston Chronical.* Houston, TX.

[3] Toffler, A., 1970. *Future Shock.* New York: Random House.

[4] *1980 Census - United States of America.* Washington, D.C.: U.S. Government Printing Office.

[5] Marshall, L.L., 1983. *Action by Design.* Washington, D.C.: American Society of Landscape Architects.

[6] Relph, E., 1976. *Place and Placelessness.* London: Pion Press.

[7] Norberg-Schulz, C., 1971. *Existence, Space and Architecture.* Washington, D.C.: Praeger Publishers.

[8] Dubos, R., 1972. *A God Within.* New York: Charles Scribners Sons.

[9] Ibid., #8.

[10] Ibid., #8.

[11] Ibid., #6.

[12] Ibid., #6.

[13] Steele, F., 1981. *Sense of Place.* Boston, MA: C.B.I. Publishing Company.

[14] Garnham, H.L., et. al., 1976. *Bandera County Study - Phase One: Upper Medina Watershed.* College Station, Tx: Texas Agricultural Extension Service.

[15] Lynch, K., 1976. *Managing the Sense of A Region.* Cambridge, MA: MIT Press.

[16] Ibid., #5.

[17] Garnham, H.L., et. al., 1972. *From the Mountain to the Sea.* Honolulu, HI: State of Hawaii.

[18] Febland, D.W. and P.A. Ritchie, 1974. *Along the Old Coach Road.* Charlottesville, VA: Division of Landscape Architecture, University of Virginia.

[19] Cullen, G. and F. MacManus, 1967. *Tenterden Explored.* Maidstone, Kent, G.B.: Kent County Council.

[20] Garnham, H.L., 1980. *What's So Special About Navasota?* Baton Rouge: The New American Landscape Press.

[21] Ibid., #17.

[22] Spirn, A.W., 1984. *The Granite Garden.* New York: Basic Books, Inc.

[23] McHarg, I.L., 1969. *Design with Nature.* Garden City, NY: Doubleday and Company, Inc.

[24] Lynch, K., 1960. *The Image of the City.* Cambridge, MA: MIT Press/Harvard Univ. Press.

[25] Perin, C., 1970. *With Man in Mind.* Cambridge, MA: MIT Press.

[26] Ibid., #20.

[27] Lynch, K., 1972. *What Time is this Place?* Cambridge, MA: MIT Press.

[28] Cullen, G., 1968. *Notation - The Observant Layman's Code for His Environment.* London: Raithby, Lawrence and Company, Ltd.

[29] Worskett, R., 1969. *The Character of Towns - An Approach to Conservation.* London: The Architectural Press.

[30] Lynch, K., and V. Pratt, 1973. *Looking at the Vineyard.* Martha's Vineyard, MA: Vineyard Open Land Foundation.

[31] Sitte, C., G. Collins, and C. Collins, 1965. *The Architecture of Towns and Cities.* New York: Columbia University Press.

[32] Sekler, E., 1963. *Historic Urban Spaces.* Cambridge, MA: Harvard Graduate School of Design.

[33] Ibid., #32.

[34] Whyte, W., 1980. *The Social Life of Small Urban Spaces.* Washington, D.C.: Conservation Foundation.

[35] Zuker, P., 1970. *Town and Square.* Cambridge, MA: MIT Press.

[36] Ashimara, Y., 1983. *The Aesthetic Townscape.* Cambridge, MA: MIT Press.

[37] Cullen, G., 1961. *Townscape.* London: Architectural Review Press.

[38] Garnham, H.L. and S. Udall, 1972. *Shaping the Future of Hawaii's Environment.* Honolulu, HI: State of Hawaii.

[39] Lynch, K. and G. Kepes, 1972. "The Openness of Open Space," *Arts in the Environment.* London: Aidan Ellis.

[40] Bryant, M., 1976. *Zoning for Community Preservation.* Austin, TX: Texas Historical Foundation.

[41] National Association of Towns and Townships, 1981. *Township Funding Opportunities - A Guide to Federal Resources for Small Communities.* Washington, D.C.

[42] Downtown Research Development Center, 1978. *Downtown Development Districts.* New York.

suggested readings

Alexander, C., S. Ishikawa, M. Silverstein, 1977. *A Pattern Language.* New York: Oxford University Press. 1171 pages.

Arnold, H.F., 1980. *Trees in Urban Design.* New York: Van Nostrand Reinhold Company. 168 pages.

Bachelard, G., 1969. *The Poetics of Space.* Boston, MA: Beacon Press. 240 pages.

Bacon, E., 1967. *Design of Cities.* New York: Viking Press. 296 pages.

Barker, J.F., M.W. Fazio, H. Hildebrandt. *The Small Town As An Art Object.* Oxford, MS: Mississippi State University. 189 pages.

Barnett, J., 1982. *An Introduction to Urban Design.* New York: Harper and Row. 260 pages.

Berk, E., 1976. *Downtown Improvement Manual.* Chicago: ASPO Press. 734 pages.

Blake, P., 1964. *God's Own Junkyard.* New York: Holt, Rinehart & Winston. 143 pages.

Bosselman, F.P., 1978. *In the Wake of the Tourist.* Washington, D.C.: The Conservation Foundation. 278 pages.

Bryce, H., 1979. *Planning Smaller Cities.* Lexington, MA: Lexington Books. 207 pages.

Castagnoli, F., 1971. *Orthogonal Town Planning in Antiquity.* Cambridge, MA: The MIT Press. 138 pages.

Chermayeff, S., C. Alexander, 1965. *Community and Privacy.* Garden City, NY: Doubleday and Company. 255 pages.

Chermayeff, S., A. Tzonis, 1971. *Shape of Community.* Baltimore, MD: Penguin. 247 pages.

Clay, G., 1973. *Close Up: How to Read the American City.* New York: Praeger Publishers. 192 pages.

Collins, G., 1968. *Planning and Cities.* New York: George Braziller. (a continuous series)

DeCarlo, G., 1970. *Urbino.* Cambridge, MA: The MIT Press. 244 pages.

Denman, A., 1981. *Design Resource Book for Small Communities.* Ellensburg, WA: Small Towns' Institute. 97 pages.

DeWolfe, I., 1966. *The Italian Townscape.* New York: George Braziller. 180 pages.

Eliande, M., 1959. *The Sacred and the Profane.* New York: Harcourt, Brace and World, Inc. 251 pages.

Frank, F., 1973. *The Zen of Seeing.* New York: Random House. 135 pages.

Garnham, H.L., 1976. *Maintaining the Spirit of Place: A Guidebook for Citizen/Professional Participation in the Preservation and Enhancement of Small Texas Towns.* College Station, TX: Texas A&M University – Landscape Architecture. 84 pages.

Getzels, J., T. Charles (Editors), 1980. *Rural and Small Town Planning.* Chicago: Planners Press. 314 pages.

Gibberd, F., 1960. *Town Design.* New York: Praeger Publishers. 247 pages.

Goodman, R., 1971. *After the Planners.* New York: Simon and Schuster. 231 pages.

Gregory, J., D. Lewis, 1977. *Community Design: By the People.* Tokyo: Process Architecture Publishing Company. 250 pages.

Gropius, W., K. Leibrand, 1969. *Town Plan for the Development of Selb.* Cambridge, MA: The MIT Press.

Gutkind, E.A., 1965. *International History of City Development,* Vol. I-VI. New York: The Free Press. 500 pages. (a continuous series)

Hall, E.T., 1966. *The Hidden Dimension.* New York: Double Day and Company. 200 pages.

Halprin, L., 1963. *Cities.* New York: Reinhold. 224 pages.

Halprin, L., J. Burns, 1974. *Taking Part: A Workshop Approach to Collective Creativity.* Cambridge, MA: The MIT Press. 327 pages.

Handlin, O., J. Burchard, 1966. *The Historian and the City.* Cambridge, MA: The MIT Press. 299 pages.

Heckscner, A., 1977. *Open Spaces: The Life of American Cities.* New York: Harper and Row. 386 pages.

Jackson, J.B., 1972. *American Space.* New York: W.W. Norton and Company. 254 pages.

Jacobs, J., 1970. *The Economy of Cities.* New York: Vintage Books. 268 pages.

Jacobs, J., 1961. *The Life and Death of the Great American City.* New York: Random House. 458 pages.

Johnson, Johnson & Roy, Inc. 1973. *Marshall: A Plan for Preservation.* Marshall, MI: Marshall Historic Society. 84 pages.

Kepes, G., 1972. *Arts of the Environment.* New York: George Braziller. 244 pages.

Lancaster, R. A. (Editor), 1983. *Recreation Park and Open Space Standards and Guidelines.* Alexandria, VA: National Recreation and Park Association. 134 pages.

LeCorbusier, 1960. *Creation is a Patient Search.* New York: Praeger Publishers. 308 pages.

Lynch, K., 1981. *A Theory of Good City Form.* Cambridge, MA: The MIT Press. 513 pages.

Lynch, K., 1976. *Managing the Sense of a Region.* Cambridge, MA: The MIT Press. 221 pages.

Lynch, K., 1971. *Site Planning,* Second Ed. Cambridge, MA: The MIT Press. 384 pages.

Lynch, K., 1972. *What Time is This Place?* Cambridge, MA: The MIT Press. 276 pages.

Maholy-Nage, S., 1968. *Matrix of Man.* New York: Praeger Publishers. 317 pages.

Maki, F., 1964. *Investigations in Collective Form.* St. Louis, MO: Washington University. 87 pages.

Marcou, O'Leary and Assoc., 1968. *Plan and Program for the Preservation of the Viewx Carre.* New Orleans, LA: Bureau of Governmental Research. 168 pages.

Meinig, D.W. (Editor), 1979. *The Interpretation of Ordinary Landscapes.* New York: Oxford University Press. 255 pages.

Morris, A.E.J., 1974. *History of Urban Form.* New York: John Wiley and Sons. 268 pages.

Mumford, L., 1961. *The City in History.* New York: Harcourt, Brace, and World, Inc. 657 pages.

Naisbitt, J., 1982. *Megatrends.* New York: Warner Books, Inc. 290 pages.

National Trust for Historic Preservation, 1976. *A Guide to Delineating Edges of Historic Districts.* Washington, D.C.: The Preservation Press. 95 pages.

Norberg-Schulz, C., 1971. *Existence, Space and Architecture,* New York: Praeger Publishers. 120 pages.

Norberg-Schulz, C., 1979. *Genius Loci.* London: Academy Editions. 213 pages.

Proshansky, H.M., W. Ittleson, L. Rivlin, 1976. *Environmental Psychology.* New York: Holt, Rinehart and Winston. 626 pages.

Ramati, R., 1981. *How to Save Your Own Street.* Garden City, NY: Doubleday Dolphin Books. 159 pages.

Rapoport, A., 1969. *House Form and Culture.* Englewood Cliffs, NJ: Prentice-Hall, Inc. 148 pages.

Rasmussen, S., 1969. *Towns and Buildings.* Cambridge, MA: The MIT Press. 473 pages.

Reps, J., 1965. *Town Planning in Frontier America.* Princeton, NJ: Princeton Press. 473 pages.

Rudolphsky, B., 1964. *Streets for People.* Garden City, NY: Double Day. 351 pages.

Shomon, J.J., 1971. *Open Land for Urban America.* Baltimore, MD: Johns Hopkins Press. 173 pages.

Simonds, J.O., 1961. *Landscape Architecture.* New York: F.W. Dodge. 243 pages.

Spector, A., 1974. *Urban Spaces.* Greenwich, CT: New York Graphic Society. 276 pages.

Spirn, A.W., 1984. *The Granite Garden - Urban Nature and Human Design.* New York: Basic Books, Inc. 334 pages.

Spreiregen, P., 1965. *Urban Design, the Architecture of Towns and Cities.* New York: McGraw Hill. 243 pages.

Toffler, A., 1970. *Future Shock.* New York: Random House. 561 pages.

Toffler, A., 1980. *The Third Wave.* New York: William Morrow and Company. 542 pages.

Toynbee, A., 1970. *Cities on the Move.* New York: Oxford University Press. 257 pages.

Tuan, Y., 1977. *Space and Place.* Minneapolis, MN: University of Minnesota Press. 235 pages.

Tuan, Y., 1974. *Topophilia.* Englewood Cliffs, NJ: Prentice-Hall. 260 pages.

Whyte, W., 1968. *The Last Landscape.* Garden City, NY: Doubleday and Company. 376 pages.

Wingo, L. Jr., 1963. *Cities and Space.* Baltimore, MD: Johns Hopkins Press. 261 pages.

Wolfe, T., 1981. *From Bauhaus to Our House.* New York: Farrar, Straus and Giroux. 143 pages.

Wolfe, T., 1970. *Radical Chic and Mau-Mauing the Flak Catchers.* New York: Farrar, Straus and Giroux. 184 pages.

Wooshett, R., 1969. *The Character of Towns.* London: Architectural Press. 271 pages.

Ziegler, A.P., L. Alder, W. Kidney, 1975. *Revolving Funds for Historic Preservation: A Manual of Practice.* Pittsburgh, PA: Ober Park Associates, Inc. 111 pages.

Zuker, P., 1970. *Town and Square.* Cambridge, MA: The MIT Press. 285 pages

appendix

NAVASOTA MAPPING CRITERIA AND GRAPHIC EXAMPLES

VEGETATION Block by block vegetation density

- High-Trees cover major portion of block (over half)
- Medium-Trees cover about half of the block
- Low-Few trees; mostly grass
- Blocks that are primarily pavement are left blank

NATURAL FEATURE

- Essential Tree - mature tree or group of trees essential to town image; function to form space, enclose views, etc.
- Unique natural feature - natural element, because of its occurrence in the surrounding town fabric, is unusual and stands apart as an identifiable entity

NATURAL AREA

- Land showing little or no manipulation by man; as similar as possible to condition before habitation; potential wildlife habitat

LAND OWNERSHIP

- Public - city, state or federally owned land
- Quasi-public - more public than private; institutional; includes church grounds, schools, and health care facilities (hospitals and nursing homes)

LAND USE

- Commercial - includes retail, offices, banks, entertainment, & food
- Institutional - includes churches, school, & health care facilities

- Public Services - includes City Hall, Post Office, Chamber of Commerce, Municipal Building, Fire & Police
- Recreation Facilities - public
- Unbuilt Land - includes vacant lots, parking lots; not the same as natural areas; shows signs of manipulation by man

HISTORIC RESOURCES

- Designated by state or national seal; plus statue

INFRASTRUCTURE

- Parking - public lots; not on-street
- Open Space - major area of green space surrounding institutional buildings with potential for public enjoyment (visual and/or physical)
- Point specific breakdown of land use categories, especially public services

TOWN STRUCTURE

- See Lynch's *Image of the City*: edge, path, node, district, landmark
- Gateway - point at which one feels he has entered town; sense of arrival is strong

GROWTH PHASES

- Use dates which are significant in terms of growth in area and changes in land use; especially rural to urban;
- Support with library (local) and newspaper records and old photos of original town layout

TRANSPORTATION

- See Grimes County Transportation Plan for proposals

VIEW POINTS

- Panorama – unlimited view over wide area
- Vista – view of visual objective or focal point & beyond, directed by partially enclosing or framing elements
- Closed Vista – same, except view stops at focal point
- Unpleasant View – visual clutter, trash, wires, poor maintenance, unbroken paved areas, etc.
- Potential View – existing view or vista capable of being developed as a pleasant visual experience
- Glimpse – brief, hasty, partial view of landmark, focal point, or some visual objective

VIEWS

- Visual perception of visual objectives such as water, vegetation, open space, pedestrian activity and flow, significant building, towers, steeples, and skylines
- Landmark – prominent and identifying feature of a landscape; historically significant buildings or site
- Focal Point – significant building, object or feature upon which view converges

SPECIAL STREETS & PLACES

- "memorable, remarkable, different, distinctive, unusual"
- Common visual elements (according to citizen questionnaire):
    well maintained yards
    well maintained homes
    old, historic homes
    new housing areas
    churches
    clean streets
    well lighted public areas
    paved streets
    sidewalks
    facilities that encourage pedestrian/community activity
    trees / shade / enclosure / color
    good views
- Break in Fabric – edge where growth & change has created a visual change in the continuity of town fabric
- Impact of Change – specific point where visual impact of change in use, scale, form, siting, etc. is dominant and distracting

DATA MAP GRAPHIC FORMAT

18 pt. Helvetica Medium lettering

Chartpak Shading Film:

 27.6 Line 10%

 30 Line 30%

 30 Line 60%

 55 Line 70%

Data Maps to be done at 1"=800'; photograph for slides
Composites for display at 1"=400'

NATURAL MASTER LIST

- Topographic Relief
- Percent Slope
- Surface Water (include floodplain & drainage patterns)
- Vegetation (types; associations; density)
- Soil (engineering & agricultural properties)
- Geology (bedrock; ground water; mineral resources)
- Climate
- Natural Influences on Town Form
- Wildlife Habitat
- Natural Areas (as similar as possible to conditions before habitation)
- Unique Natural Features
- Natural Hazard Zones
- Ambient Qualities
- Pollution

CULTURAL MASTER LIST

- Land Ownership (private; public; quasi-public)
- Existing Public & Private Infrastructure (public buildings, services, facilities & institutions)
- Generalized Land Use & Zoning
- New Development Proposals
- Historic Resources
- Transportation Network
- Town Structure (edge, path, node, landmark, district, gateway)
- Phases of Growth
- Response to Citizen Questionnaire
- Activity Patterns

VISUAL MASTER LIST

- Views & Viewpoints (panorama, vista, glimpse, potential view, unpleasant view, closed vista) (landmark, focal point, open space, water, buildings, pedestrian activity)
- Special Places (strong sense of place)
- Special Streets (identify common elements)
- Impact of Change; Break in Fabric
- Poor Quality Streets
- Zone of Unified Visual Character
- Zone of Non-unified Visual Character
- Zone of Visual Complexity
- Visually Non-complex Zone
- Sequence of Spaces
- Enclosure

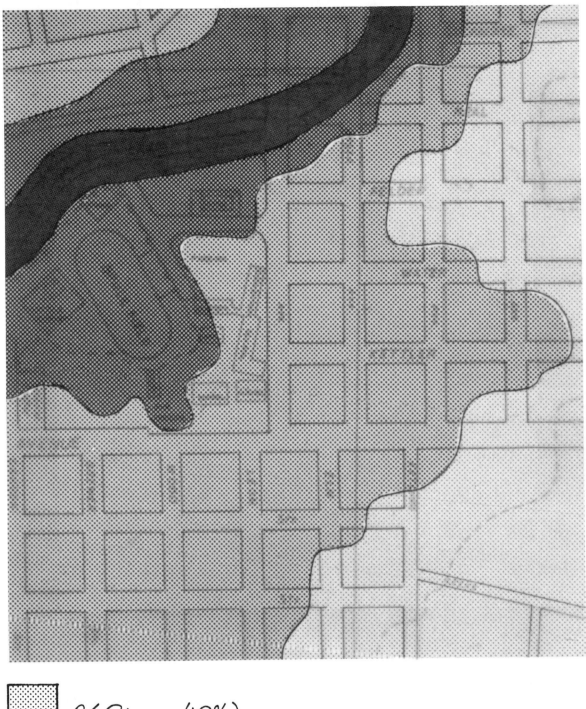

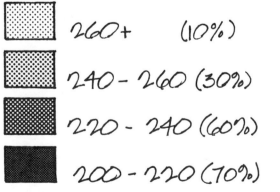 260+   (10%)

240 - 260 (30%)

220 - 240 (60%)

200 - 220 (70%)

TOPOGRAPHIC RELIEF

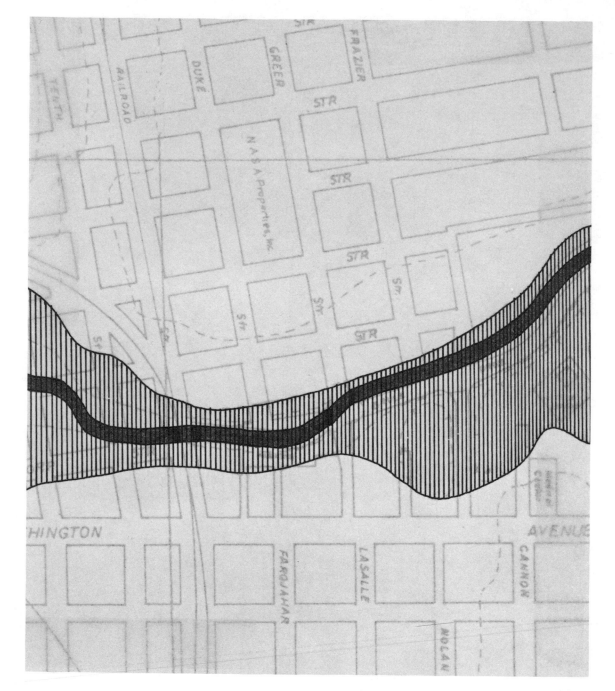

 CREEK

 FLOODPLAIN

SURFACE WATER

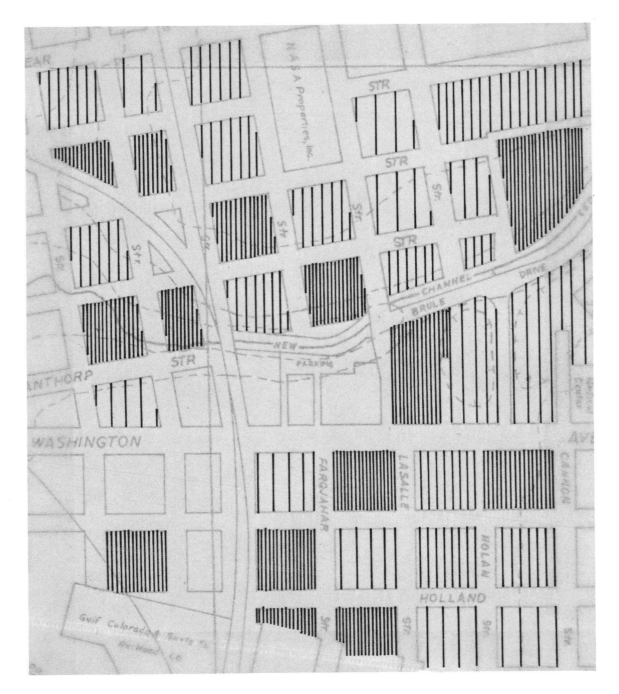

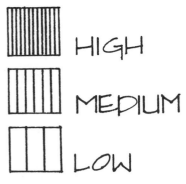 HIGH

MEDIUM

LOW

VEGETATION DENSITY *block by block tree cover*

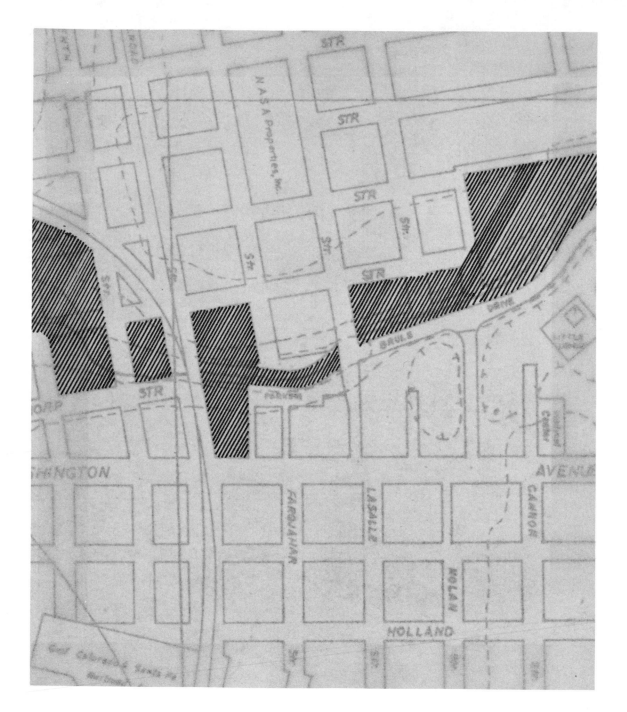

 NATURAL AREA

potential wildlife habitat
criteria: little or no manipulation by man; as simi-
          lar as possible to condition before habitation

138

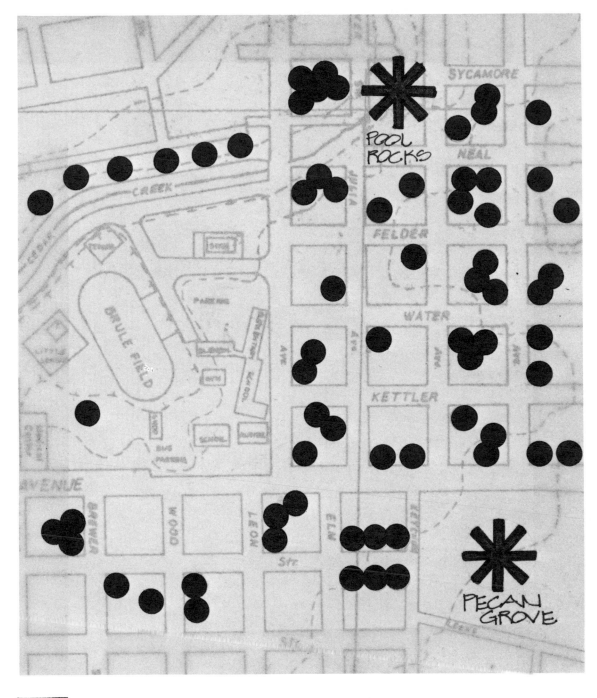

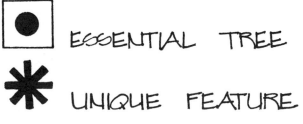
ESSENTIAL TREE

UNIQUE FEATURE

UNIQUE NATURAL FEATURE

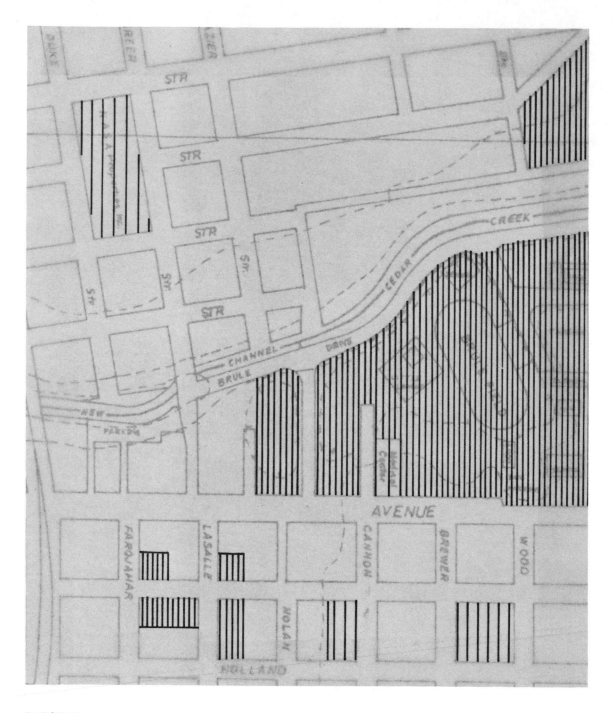

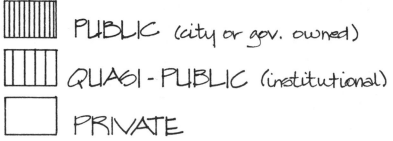

PUBLIC (city or gov. owned)

QUASI-PUBLIC (institutional)

PRIVATE

LAND OWNERSHIP

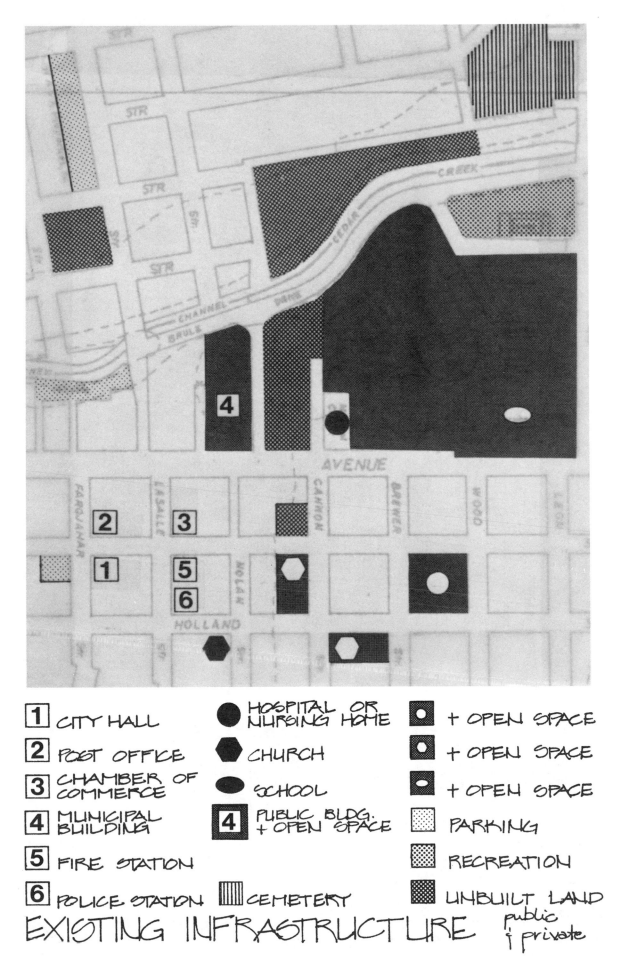

1 CITY HALL

2 POST OFFICE

3 CHAMBER OF COMMERCE

4 MUNICIPAL BUILDING

5 FIRE STATION

6 POLICE STATION

● HOSPITAL OR NURSING HOME

⬡ CHURCH

⬭ SCHOOL

4 PUBLIC BLDG. + OPEN SPACE

▥ CEMETERY

▣ + OPEN SPACE

▣ + OPEN SPACE

▪ + OPEN SPACE

⬚ PARKING

▦ RECREATION

▨ UNBUILT LAND

EXISTING INFRASTRUCTURE public & private

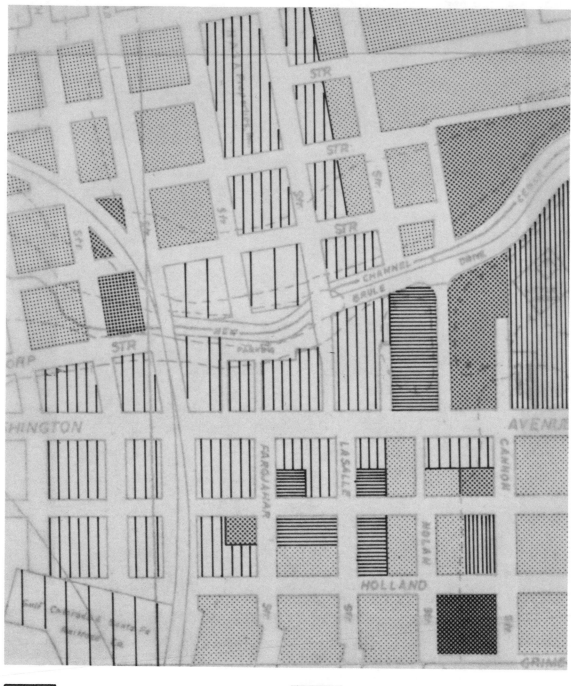

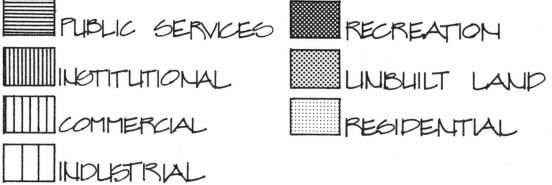

PUBLIC SERVICES   RECREATION

INSTITUTIONAL   UNBUILT LAND

COMMERCIAL   RESIDENTIAL

INDUSTRIAL

GENERALIZED LAND USE (block by block where possible)

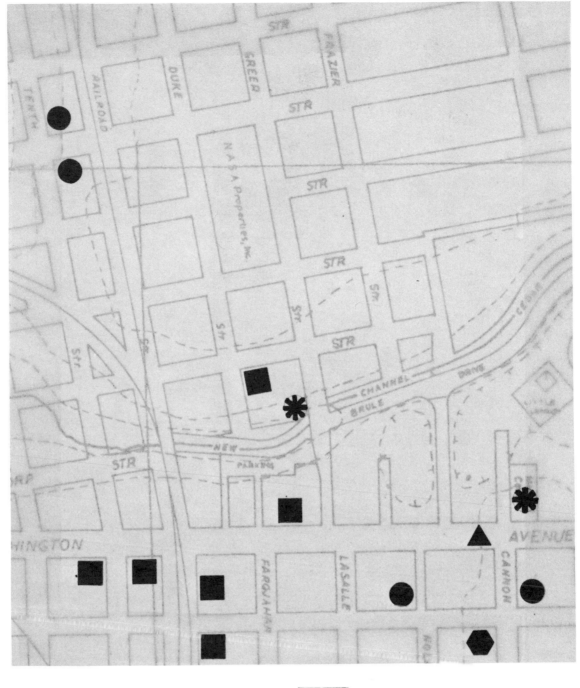

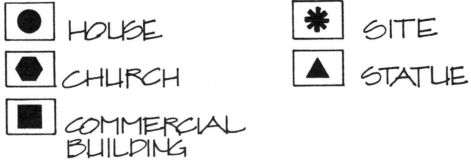

⬤ HOUSE	✳ SITE
⬣ CHURCH	▲ STATUE
◼ COMMERCIAL BUILDING	

HISTORIC RESOURCES

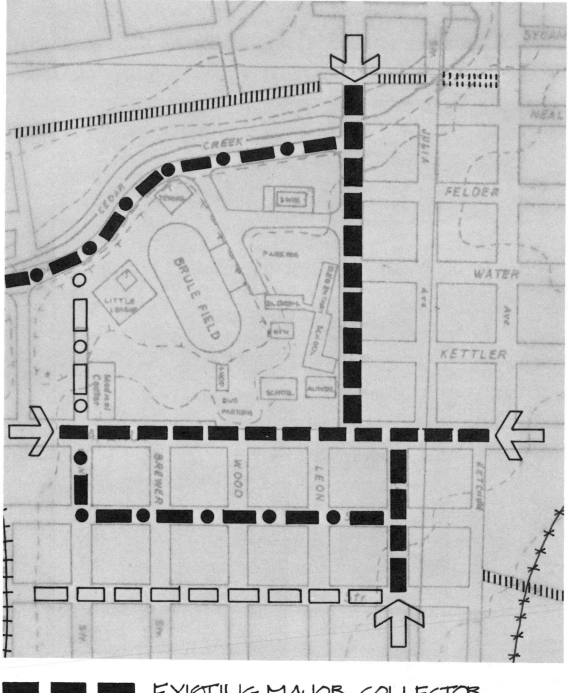

■ ■■ ■	EXISTING MAJOR COLLECTOR
☐ ☐ ☐	PROPOSED MAJOR COLLECTOR
■ ● ■	EXISTING MINOR ARTERIAL
☐ ○ ☐	PROPOSED MINOR ARTERIAL
‖‖‖‖/‖‖‖‖	UNPAVED STREET/R.O.W. ONLY
++++/××××	RAILROAD/ABANDONED

TRANSPORTATION NETWORK

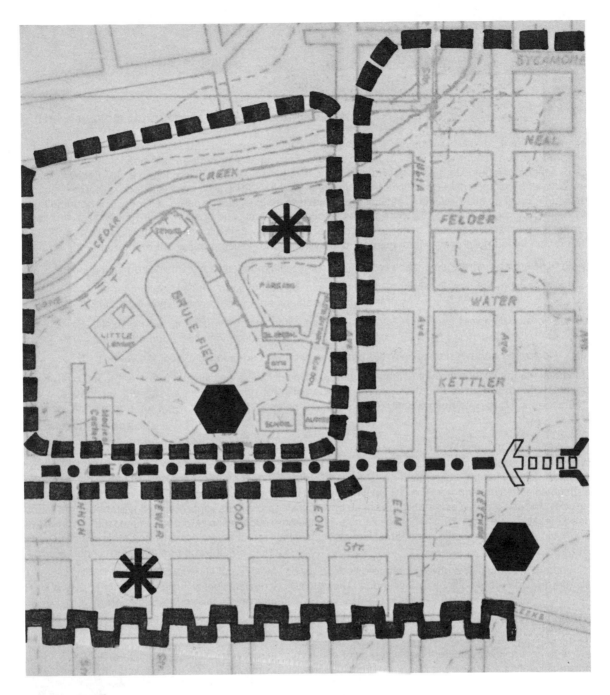

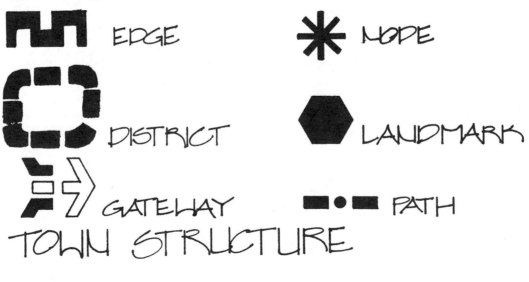

EDGE   ✳ NODE

DISTRICT   ⬣ LANDMARK

GATEWAY   ▬ ● ▬ PATH

TOWN STRUCTURE

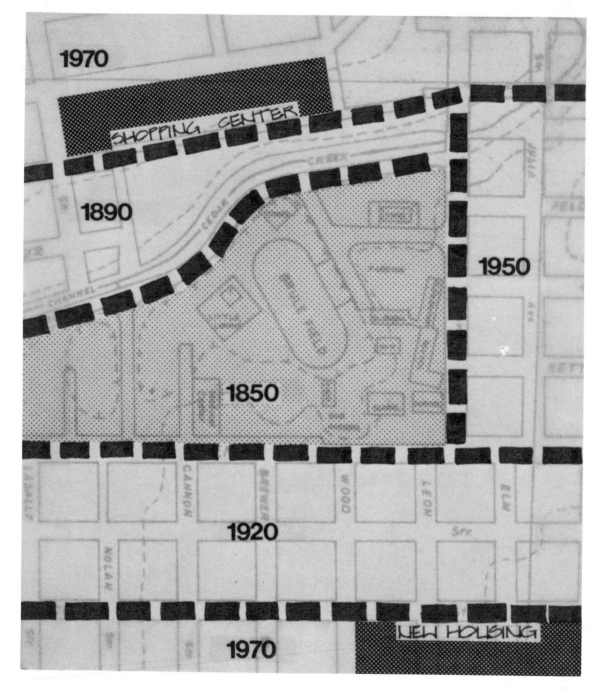

1970

SHOPPING CENTER

CREEK

1890

1950

1850

1920

NEW HOUSING

1970

 ORIGINAL TOWN LAYOUT

PROPOSED NEW DEVELOPMENT

PHASES OF GROWTH

146

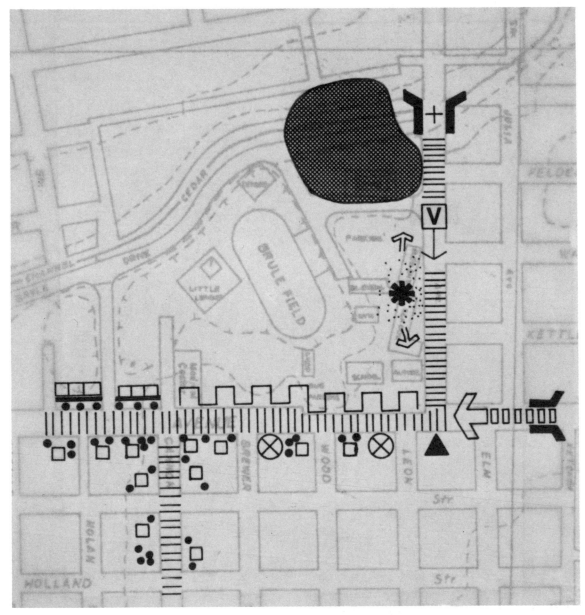

▨ SPECIAL PLACE	✳	GATHERING PLACE
‖‖‖‖ SPECIAL STREET	⸪	PEDESTRIAN ACTIVITY
[V]→ GOOD VIEW	▲	FOCAL POINT
⅄+ ENTRY POINT	●	ESSENTIAL TREE
⊏⊐▷ GATEWAY	▬	SIDEWALK
⊓⊔ BREAK IN FABRIC	☐	BUILDINGS · HOUSES · CHURCHES · IMPORTANT TO IMAGE
⊗ IMPACT OF CHANGE		

SPECIAL STREETS & PLACES

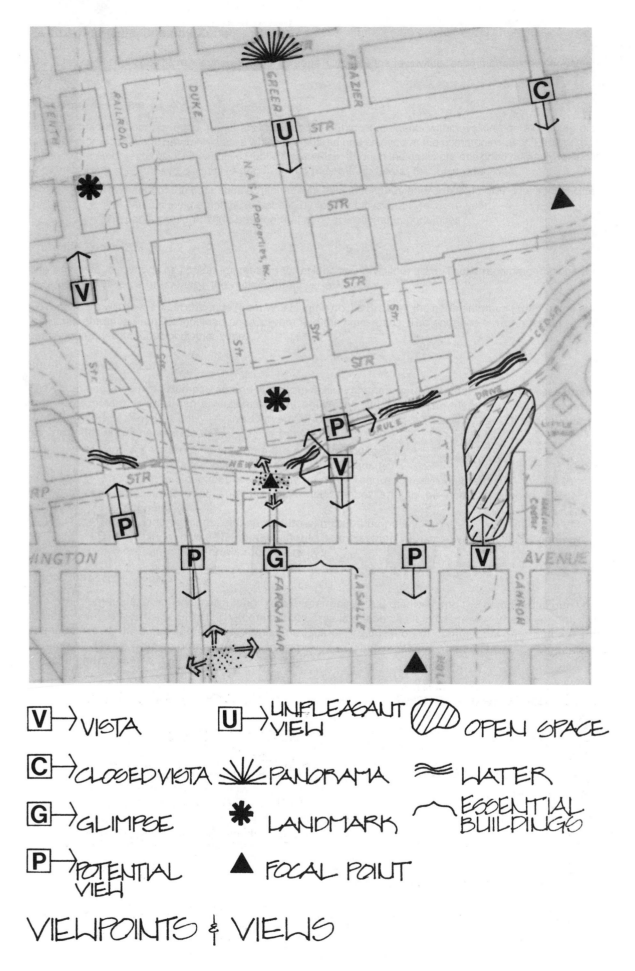

V→ VISTA	U→ UNPLEASANT VIEW	OPEN SPACE
C→ CLOSED VISTA	PANORAMA	WATER
G→ GLIMPSE	* LANDMARK	ESSENTIAL BUILDINGS
P→ POTENTIAL VIEW	▲ FOCAL POINT	

VIEWPOINTS & VIEWS

What do you think about Navasota?

The Navasota Examiner

And Grimes County Review

Serving Texas' 5th Largest Dairy Farming County — The Land of Milk and Honey

VOLUME 81   EIGHTEEN PAGES   THURSDAY, JULY 14, 1977   20 CENTS   NUMBER 47

Have you ever said, "I wish someone would ask me what I think; I'd tell them!" Well, here is your chance.

Navasota is being studied for the purpose of preparing a Townscape Preservation and Enhancement Plan by The New American Landscape firm of College Station through a National Endowment for the Arts grant. The goal of the study is to protect the important aspects of Navasota's image.

The following questions are part of an effort to obtain the opinions of the citizens of Navasota about how the town looks and how they would like it to be changed.

Your cooperation in answering these questions will help make Navasota a more enjoyable place to live and work. A box will be provided in the lobby of City Hall for collecting completed questionnaires. The box will be picked up on Tuesday, July 26, for tabulation of the responses.

1. What do you think is special about Navasota?

_____

_____

_____

_____

2. If you could change anything about Navasota, what would it be?

_____

_____

_____

3. What are the things you hope never change in Navasota?

_____

_____

4. When showing out-of-town guests the sights of Navasota, what places in Navasota would you be sure to show them?

_____

_____

_____

_____

5. In your opinion, what are the three most attractive streets in Navasota?

_____

_____

_____

6. What things do you think make a neighborhood nice?

_____

_____

_____

7. What improvements would you like to see made in the downtown area of Navasota?

_____

_____

_____

_____

A longer questionnaire, used in a meeting with the Citizens Advisory Committee of Navasota, is available to interested citizens or organizations from David Dickson, Community Development Specialist, at City Hall. Your further participation is encouraged.
July 12, 1977

ave you ever said, "I wish they would ask me what I thought; I'd tell them!"

This is your chance! Navasota is being analyzed for the purpose of undertaking a townscape preservation and enhancement planning project, the goal of which is to protect the important aspects of town image.

This activity is an effort to collect and synthesize the opinions of the citizenry in order to better understand their values and standards concerning how the town looks, how they use its public areas and how they feel about its future growth and change.

Your cooperation will aid in making Navasota a more enjoyable place to live and work.

1. What age group are you in:

   0-18 ____ , 18-25 ____ , 25-60____ , 60 and over ____ .

2. What is your occupation?_____

   Where is your work located?_____

   Downtown _____ , in the residential areas of town _____ , on the edge of out of town_____ .

3. In which quadrant of Navasota do you live?

   Northwest_____ , Northeast_____ , Southwest_____ , Southeast_____ , Out of town_____ .

4. How long have you lived in Navasota?_____

   Do you consider yourself a "Newcomer"_____ or an "Oldtimer"_____ ?

5. If you are not a native Navasotian, for what reason did you move to Navasota? (mark as many as are applicable):

   ____Employment   ____To be in a small Texas town

   ____To be away from larger cities   ____Happen to find a house here

   ____To be closer to larger cities   ____For the life style and sense

   ____For its proximity to historic   of place

   sites   ____For the agricultural orienta-

   ____Other (specify)_____   tion

6. Do you have school age children?   Yes____ , No____

   If "Yes" list ages, school attending, distance from school and method of transportation to school:

   _____

   _____

7. What are your favorite forms of recreation and where are they located?

_____

_____

8. Where do you take your family for outings such as picnics?

_____

_____

9. When you walk what is the purpose? (mark as many as are applicable):
   As a means of transportation_____, for health reasons_____,
   for recreation_____.

10. Is there anything characteristic or distinctive about Navasota which
    would set it apart from other towns its size in Texas?

_____

_____

11. If you could change anything about Navasota, what would it be?

_____

_____

12. What are the things you hope never change in Navasota?_____

_____

13. When coming to Navasota from Anderson where do you feel that you have
    entered the community of Navasota?_____

_____

14. When coming to Navasota from Hempstead where do you feel that you have
    entered the community of Navasota?_____

_____

15. When coming to Navasota from Washington on the Brazos where do you feel
    that you have entered the community of Navasota?_____

_____

16. When coming to Navasota from College Station where do you feel that you
    have entered the community of Navasota?_____

_____

17. Which of the major routes coming into Navasota do you find most
    pleasing? Why?_____

_____

18. Which of the major routes coming into Navasota do you find most un-
    pleasant? Why?_____

_____

19. When showing an out of town guest the sights of Navasota what places would you want to be sure to show him?_____

    _____

20. What areas would you be sure not to show your guests?_____

    _____

21. Where are your favorite views of Navasota or the surrounding country-side?_____

    _____

22. In your opinion what are the three most attractive streets in Navasota?

    _____

    _____

23. In your opinion what are the three nicest neighborhoods in Navasota?

    _____

    _____

24. What things do you think make a neighborhood nice?_____

    _____

25. Are there any parts of the community of Navasota in which you feel uncomfortable or unwelcome? Which ones and why?_____

    _____

26. Do you enjoy being out at night in Navasota? Yes____, No____
    Is the lighting adequate? Yes____, No____
    What areas do you feel are in most need of improved lighting?_____

    _____

27. What time of day do you prefer outdoor activities - does this vary with with the seasons?
    SEASON   TIME(S) OF DAY
    Spring_____
    Summer_____
    Fall_____
    Winter_____

28. Would you like to see tourists attracted to Navasota? Yes____, No____

29. If "Yes" what sort of facilities would you feel would need to be provided?_____

    _____

30. What building and/or areas in Navasota do you feel are of historic value?_____

    _____

31. What is your opinion of the following community services in Navasota?

TOO MUCH   TOO FEW   ENOUGH

_____   _____   _____   Housing

_____   _____   _____   Variety of retail establishments

_____   _____   _____   Adult education programs

_____   _____   _____   Facilities encouraging pedestrian travel

_____   _____   _____   Open space such as parks, etc.

_____   _____   _____   Recreational diversity

_____   _____   _____   Cultural experience such as museums,
                                        theatre

_____   _____   _____   Public gathering places

_____   _____   _____   Public sport and athletic facilities

_____   _____   _____   Medical evidence

TOO MUCH   TOO FEW   ENOUGH

_____   _____   _____   Youth activities

_____   _____   _____   Civic organization

_____   _____   _____   Citizen involvement in city planning
                                        projects

_____   _____   _____   Facilities for senior citizens

32. What changes would you like to see made in the community services of
Navasota?_____

_____

33. How often do you come to Downtown Navasota?

Daily____, 4-6 days per week____, 1-3 days per week____, once a week___.

34. For what purpose(s) do you come to Downtown Navasota? (mark as many as
are applicable):

____Work   ____Recreation

____Business appointments   ____Dining

____Services, repairs, etc.   ____To see what is happening

____School   ____"Cruising"

____To visit friends   ____Other (specify)_____

_____

35. To which places in Downtown Navasota do you most often go?_____

_____

_____

36. What form of transportation do you normally use to get Downtown Navasota? _____

37. When you drive to Downtown Navasota where do you park? _____
    _____
    Is this the best parking place? Yes____, No____, Why? _____
    _____

38. Is the railroad in Downtown Navasota an inconvenience? Yes____, No_____
    If "Yes" do you have any solutions to suggest _____

39. What is your opinion of the use of buildings and land space in the existing Downtown areas of Navasota?

    TOO MANY   TOO FEW   ENOUGH
    _____   _____   _____ Shops
    _____   _____   _____ Business offices
    _____   _____   _____ Restaurants
    _____   _____   _____ Bars
    _____   _____   _____ Governmental

    TOO MANY   TOO FEW   ENOUGH
    _____   _____   _____ Parking
    _____   _____   _____ Religious (churches, etc.)
    _____   _____   _____ Residential
    _____   _____   _____ Hotel and motels
    _____   _____   _____ Cultural (museums, etc.)
    _____   _____   _____ Recreational
    _____   _____   _____ Parks and other open spaces
    _____   _____   _____ Medical and pharmaceutical
    _____   _____   _____ Industrial
    _____   _____   _____ Other (specify)_____
    _____

40. How has the Downtown area of Navasota changed since you have lived here? _____
    _____

41. What improvements would you like to see made in the Downtown area of Navasota? _____
    _____

42. What would you like the Downtown image of Navasota to be?_____
_____

43. What kinds of stores would you like and feel most appropriate to be in
    Downtown Navasota? (mark as many as are applicable):

    ____ Grocery store   ____ Clothing specialties
    ____ Chain food store   ____ Dept. store chain (i.e., Dillards,
    ____ Gourmet store   Foleys)
    ____ Delicatessen   ____ Retail marts, discount chains (i.e.,
    ____ Liquor store   Globe)
    ____ Bakery   ____ Furniture and home furnishings
    ____ Drugstore   ____ Fast service restaurant (i.e., Sonic)
    ____ Shoes   ____ More services and repairs
    ____ Sporting equipment   ____ Real estate agency
    ____ Book store   ____ Equipment and building materials
    ____ Hardware store   ____ Automotive dealers
    ____ Crafts shop   ____ Health food store
    ____ Jewelry shop   ____ Flowers and plant store
    ____ Bicycle shop   ____ Outlet for local "homemade" goods
    ____ Other (specify)_____
    _____

44. Do you regularly shop in Downtown Navasota? Yes____, No____
    If "Yes" why?_____
    _____

45. Do you shop elsewhere? Yes____, No____
    If "Yes" where?_____
    How often do you shop elsewhere_____

46. Do you prefer this other place to Downtown Navasota? Yes____, No____
    If "Yes" what makes this other place better?_____
    _____

47. In your opinion where do most of the Downtown Navasota shoppers come
    from?
    ____ Within walking distance of Downtown Navasota
    ____ Other parts of Navasota (specify)_____
    ____ Other communities around Navasota
    ____ Tourist and recreation areas
    ____ Rural areas around Navasota

48. Which of the following forms of citizen involvement would you find most agreeable? Mark your first three preferences (1, 2, and 3):

____ Block representative and block meetings

____ Personal interview by door-to-door survey

____ Community workshops

____ Public meetings

____ Official public hearings

____ Completion of questionnaire distributed in newspaper

____ Street interviews with random sampling of citizens

____ Civic organization made up of existing club representatives

____ Leave it up to your elected officials

____ No participation

49. How would you have changed this questionnaire to make it better?

_____

_____

index